Math Games
Grades 5–6

Author: Joyce A. Stulgis-Blalock

Editors: Mary Dieterich and Sarah M. Anderson

Proofreader: Margaret Brown

COPYRIGHT © 2011 Mark Twain Media, Inc.

ISBN 978-1-58037-567-2

Printing No. CD-404152

Mark Twain Media, Inc., Publishers
Distributed by Carson-Dellosa Publishing LLC

Visit us at www.carsondellosa.com

Table of Contents

Introduction to the Teacher iv
Directions for Playing Math Games 1

Unit 1: Place Value 2
Organize Ones, Tens, and Hundreds 2
Place Value Race 3
Bag Some Huge Numbers 4
Grab Base Ten Number
    Representations 5
Pull in Some Place Value 6
Ensnare Some Big Numbers 7
Roll in Tricky Place Value 8
Wangle Some Big Whole Numbers 9

Unit 2: Addition and Subtraction 10
Chalk Up a Sum 10
Catch the Sum 11
Grabbing More Than and Less Than
    Answers 12
Drag in Addition Estimation 13
Rope Some Averages 14
Rescue Inverse Operations 15
Claim a Difference 16
Gain a Difference 17
Peg Subtraction Answers 18

Unit 3: Multiplication and Division 19
Score With Multiples of 3 and 4 19
Nab Multiples of 5 and 6 20
Conquer Big Multiples 21
Snag a Big Multiple 22
Grasp the Inverse Operation 23
Haul in Some Inverse Operations 24
Charge for the Quotient 25
A Quotient Sprint 26
Cart Off Some Quotients 27
Grapple for Some Quotients 28
Dive Into Challenging Division 29

Unit 4: Decimals 30
Decimal Dash 30
Drag in Decimals on a Number Line 31
Nab a Product 32
Snare Decimal Multiples 33
Snap Up Change 34

Earn Some Decimals 35
Get Ready to Nab Decimals on a
    Number Line 36
Swoop Up Rounding Decimals 37
Reap Rounding Decimals to the
    Hundredths 38
Rack Up Rounding Decimals to the
    Thousandths 39
Sweep Up Decimals 40
Tag Some Ordered Decimals 41
Ambush Some Decimal Round-ups 42
Dive for Decimal Quotient Unknowns 43
Extract Some Decimal Division
    Estimates 44
Groove With Decimal Multiples 45

Unit 5: Factors 46
Factor Find 46
Grapple With Greatest Common
    Factors (GCF) 47

Unit 6: Fractions 48
Clip Lowest Common Denominators 48
Conquest Over Common
    Denominators 49
Find an Improper Fraction 50
Hook Fractions as Part of a
    Collection 51
Lasso Fractions in a Collection 52
Reduce Those Fractions! 53
Snatch the Least Common Multiple 54
Secure Some Fractions 55
Grasp a Fractional Location 56
Stamp Out Common Denominators 57
Triumph Over Adding Fractions 58
Bring in a Flood of Quotients 59
Win a Product 60
Conquer Multiplying Mixed Numbers 61
Finding Fractional Parts of Whole
    Numbers 62

**Unit 7: Fraction, Decimal, and Percent
    Equivalents** 63
Button Down Fractions and Decimals ... 63

Table of Contents (cont.)

Strike Out Some Mixed Numbers..........64
Finding Fraction-Decimal Equivalents...65
Grab on to Fraction-Decimal-Percent
    Equivalents 66
Collar Some Multiples 67
Salvage Lots of Percent Equivalents.....68

Unit 8: Percents **69**
Pounce on a Percent.............................69
Round Up Percents................................70
Snare Sale Prices 71
Tag the Percent One Number Is of
    Another Number 72
Wrap Up a Raise 73

Unit 9: Ratios **74**
Draw in Ratios.......................................74
Rack Up Ratios 75

Unit 10: Positive and Negative
Numbers...**76**
Conquer Positive and Negative
    Numbers...76
Mark Some Positive and Negative
    Numbers 77
Pocket Positive and Negative
    Solutions 78

Unit 11: Algebra **79**
Hook Some Patterns 79
Pick Up a Numerical Pattern 80
Nab an Expression.................................81
Dance Away With Algebraic
    Expressions 82
Peg Some Algebraic Equations.............83
Glide Through Algebraic Equations.......84
Hook Algebraic Unknowns 85
Zip Away With Algebraic Expressions...86

Unit 12: Properties............................**87**
Button Down the Commutative
    Property 87
Draw in the Distributive Property..........88
Douse the Density Property 89

Unit 13: Exponents, Square Roots, and
Proportions **90**
Overcome Exponents............................90
Latch on to Square Root Estimations....91
Search for a Square Root 92
Strike Out Square Roots 93
Pounce on Proportions..........................94

Unit 14: Measurement **95**
Crunch Customary Units.......................95
Swap Customary Units..........................96
Tackle Metric Measurement 97
Munch Some Metrics 98

Unit 15: Geometry.............................**99**
Lasso Lines and Points 99
Search for the Geometric Gold 100
Play With Perimeters 101
Buffalo Some Triangular Perimeters....102
Reach for Rectangular Areas..............103
Latch on to Areas 104
Latch on to Two-Dimensional Areas....105
Crunch the Area of Triangles..............106
Dive Into Triangular Areas 107
Conquer Geometric Shapes 108
Stamp Out Surface Areas 109
Wangle Surface Areas 110
Volley for Volume.................................111
Snatch Geometric Patterns.................112
Grapple Geometric Patterns 113
Master Coordinates.............................114
Grab a Coordinate..............................115

Unit 16: Data Analysis and
Probability......................................**116**
Grip Some Graphing 116
Lap Up Laps.......................................117

Answer Keys **118**

Introduction to the Teacher

These math games were developed over the past several years. Students in many grade levels have tried them and have really enjoyed playing them. Activities are arranged by skill level and topic and are progressively more difficult, making this book ideal for differentiated classrooms. Activities build on knowledge covered earlier in the book, encouraging students to focus on concept development.

Since reading comprehension and the use of reasoning are skills being assessed in most state and national standardized tests, this book will help students master those critical thinking and balanced literacy skills.

The games were designed to reinforce the National Council of Teachers of Mathematics (NCTM) Standards. The standards that pertain to each game are noted at the top of each page.

The games are unique because they incorporate several skills. They are not only math "skills" games, but are also games of "strategy." The students must have good math knowledge, but they must also be thinking of where they want to move in the answer boxes with their next solution to achieve three boxes in a row.

Each game can be used for small or whole groups. Here are some ways in which the games may be played:

1. Students can be given a page as a morning practice sheet.
2. They can play the games as a race, to see who finishes first.
3. The pages can be used as test preparation.
4. They can be played with partners or in teams of three.
5. If the teacher makes a transparency of a game, it can be played with competing teams within the class.
   (More detailed directions follow this page.)

I hope this book will help you and your students.

Directions for Playing Math Games

To play the games individually as a review, a learning exercise, or as a morning warm-up exercise:

1. First, the teacher chooses the skill he/she wants the students to practice.
2. Copies of the chosen game are made for each student.
3. The games are passed out facedown on the students' desks.
4. When the teacher says, "Go," the students turn over the game, and they begin to match answers in the boxes on the page to the problems listed.
5. They write the number of the item or problem on the line provided in the box that has the correct answer. They must then cross out the number of the problem they have solved. When the whole class has finished, the teacher calls out the answers, and the students correct their own work, or they can exchange with a partner, and the partner can correct the game.

To play the games in teams of 2 or 3 players:

1. The teacher chooses the skill the students need to practice.
2. Copies of the chosen game are made for every two or three students.
3. The class is divided into teams of two or three students, and it is determined who will go first, second, and third.
4. The teacher passes out the games facedown, one game per team.
5. When the teacher says, "Go," the students turn over the game.
6. The student who goes first chooses any problem listed on the page to complete. If the answer is correct, or the other player(s) agree with the answer, the first player puts his/her initials and the problem number in the answer box and <u>crosses out the question</u>. If the answer is NOT correct, that student loses a turn. Right or wrong, the game paper passes to student number two. After student number two finishes, the game passes to student number three, and so the game continues.
7. The person who gets any three answer boxes in a row wins. Each answer box can only be used one time for a win. The game can continue until all of the boxes are claimed or until a win is no longer possible.

To play the games as a whole-class activity:

1. The teacher chooses the game and then makes a transparency of it.
2. The class is divided into teams of three or four students each. Each team should be represented by a name or number.
3. The teacher places the transparency on the overhead projector.
4. The teacher explains to the class that the problems are listed on the page, and the answers are in the boxes on the page.
5. The teacher then states that he/she will call out the number of a problem; for example, he/she announces: "Number 5."
6. The first person to raise his/her hand, or the person the teacher calls upon, will state the answer to Number 5. If it is correct, then that team claims that answer box, and the team's name or number and the problem number are placed in that box. The teacher then <u>crosses out the problem</u> that has been solved, so the students will not attempt to solve it again.
7. The winner is either the team with the most boxes or the team that claims three boxes in a row; the teacher can make the choice.

Name: _____ Date: _____

UNIT 1

Organize Ones, Tens, and Hundreds

422 ___	721 ___	372 ___
370 ___	234 ___	730 ___
543 ___	724 ___	324 ___
242 ___	542 ___	722 ___
302 ___	230 ___	723 ___

Determine the number represented by each statement below, and find the corresponding number in the boxes above. Write the item number on the line in the box that has the correct answer.

1. 3 tens, 2 hundreds, 4 ones
2. 4 ones, 3 hundreds, 2 tens
3. 5 hundreds, 3 ones, 4 tens
4. 5 hundreds, 2 ones, 4 tens
5. 2 ones, 4 hundreds, 2 tens
6. 2 hundreds, 4 tens, 2 ones
7. 7 tens, 2 ones, 3 hundreds
8. 7 hundreds, 4 ones, 2 tens
9. 2 tens, 7 hundreds, 3 ones
10. 7 hundreds, 0 ones, 3 tens
11. 3 hundreds, 2 ones, 0 tens
12. 2 tens, 7 hundreds, 1 one
13. 0 ones, 7 tens, 3 hundreds
14. 2 tens, 7 hundreds, 2 ones
15. 2 hundreds, 0 ones, 3 tens

Name: _____ Date: _____

NCTM Standard: Number and Operations – understand numbers and ways of representing numbers

Place Value Race

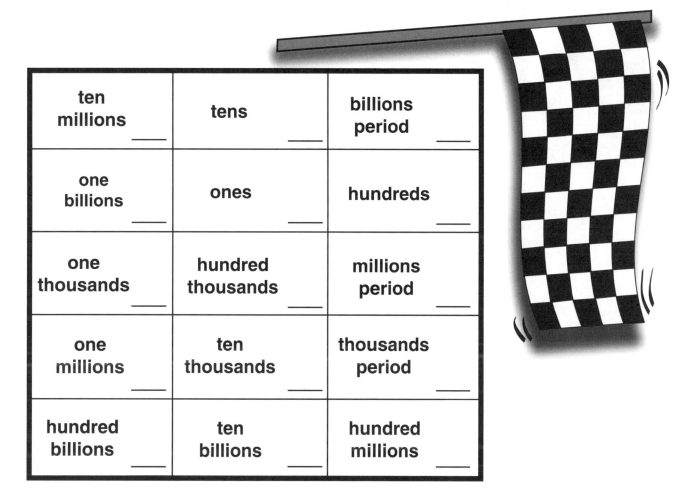

For each number below, tell the place value of the underlined and bolded number(s), and find the value in the boxes above. Write the item number on the line in the box that has the correct answer.

1. 300,459,342,**7**54

2. 21,29**5**

3. 1**5**2,985

4. **4**50,001,978

5. 7**8**,000,230

6. **3**,598

7. 3**8**9,450,820

8. 7**6**3,700,340,800

9. 52,**7**00,203

10. 29**5**,700,280,121

11. **221**,000

12. **600**,289,001

13. 2,0**1**8

14. **9**95,999,901,891

15. **402**,767,021,671

NCTM Standard: Number and Operations – understand the place-value structure of the base ten system

Bag Some Huge Numbers

400,002 ___	40,020 ___	818,320 ___
444,002 ___	402,202 ___	83,002 ___
800,004 ___	83,020 ___	420,040 ___
823,045 ___	420,002 ___	80,020 ___
812,032 ___	803,052 ___	403,020 ___

Read the words below, and then find the numbers represented by the words in the boxes above. Write the item number on the line in the box that has the correct answer.

1. four hundred thousand, two
2. four hundred twenty thousand, two
3. four hundred two thousand, two hundred two
4. eight hundred eighteen thousand, three hundred twenty
5. eight hundred thousand, four
6. four hundred twenty thousand, forty
7. eight hundred twelve thousand, thirty-two
8. four hundred three thousand, twenty
9. eight hundred three thousand, fifty-two
10. four hundred forty-four thousand, two
11. eight hundred twenty-three thousand, forty-five
12. forty thousand, twenty
13. eighty thousand, twenty
14. eighty-three thousand, twenty
15. eighty-three thousand, two

Name: _____ Date: _____

NCTM Standard: Number and Operations – understand the place-value structure of the base ten system

UNIT 1

Grab Base Ten
Number Representations

572 ___	542 ___	551 ___	249 ___
232 ___	253 ___	537 ___	555 ___
229 ___	265 ___	543 ___	583 ___
228 ___	261 ___	532 ___	238 ___

Determine the number represented in expanded form below, and then find the answer in the boxes above. Write the item number on the line in the box that has the correct answer.

1. 3 ones, 2 hundreds, 5 tens   **2.** 2 hundreds, 3 tens, 2 ones

3. 4 tens, 3 ones, 5 hundreds   **4.** 2 ones, 5 hundreds, 4 tens

5. 8 ones, 2 hundreds, 3 tens   **6.** 4 tens, 9 ones, 2 hundreds

7. 5 tens, 5 ones, 5 hundreds   **8.** 2 tens, 2 hundreds, 8 ones

9. 1 one, 6 tens, 2 hundreds   **10.** 6 tens, 2 hundreds, 5 ones

11. 7 tens, 5 hundreds, 2 ones   **12.** 7 ones, 3 tens, 5 hundreds

13. 1 one, 5 hundreds, 5 tens   **14.** 3 tens, 5 hundreds, 2 ones

15. 8 tens, 3 ones, 5 hundreds   **16.** 9 ones, 2 tens, 2 hundreds

Name: _____ Date: _____

NCTM Standard: Number and Operations – understand the place-value structure of the base ten system

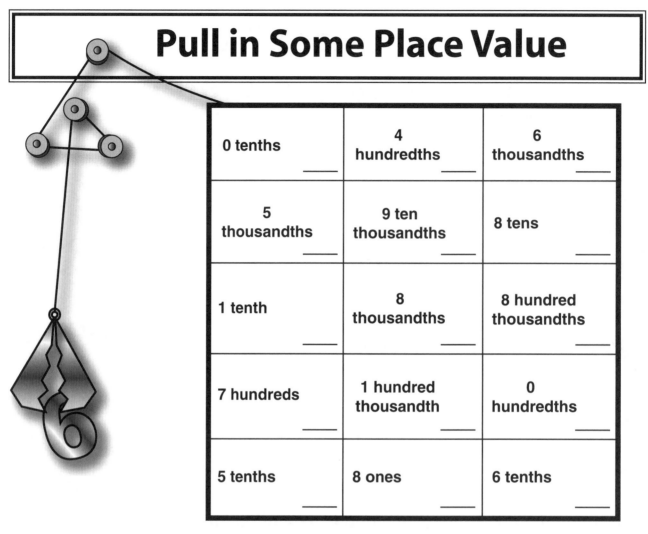

Pull in Some Place Value

0 tenths ____	4 hundredths ____	6 thousandths ____
5 thousandths ____	9 ten thousandths ____	8 tens ____
1 tenth ____	8 thousandths ____	8 hundred thousandths ____
7 hundreds ____	1 hundred thousandth ____	0 hundredths ____
5 tenths ____	8 ones ____	6 tenths ____

Determine the place value of the underlined digits below, and find the answer in the boxes above. Write the item number on the line in the box that has the correct answer.

1.   1.34<u>5</u>8
2.   5.268<u>9</u>
3.   63.2900<u>1</u>
4. 102.<u>5</u>76
5.   7<u>8</u>.2509
6.   2.2000<u>8</u>
7.   5.1<u>0</u>987
8.   61.34<u>5</u>
9.   <u>8</u>1.3450
10.   0.79<u>8</u>63
11.   7.<u>6</u>5931
12. <u>7</u>07.12
13.   4.2<u>0</u>986
14.   51.<u>0</u>981
15. 786.34<u>6</u>901

Name: _____ Date: _____

NCTM Standard: Number and Operations – understand the place-value structure of the base ten system

Ensnare Some Big Numbers

Determine the large number represented by the dots in each place below, and find the matching number in the boxes below. Write the item number on the line in the box that has the correct answer.

	millions				thousands				ones		
	H	T	O		H	T	O		H	T	O
1.											
2.											
3.											
4.											
5.											
6.											
7.											
8.											
9.											
10.											
11.											
12.											

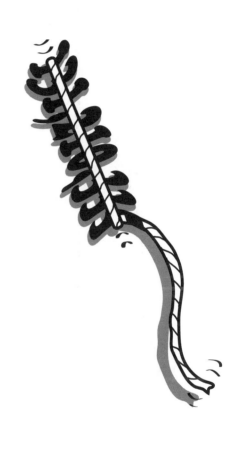

321,121,311 ___	131,012,135 ___	311,121,301 ___	312,121,304 ___
132,300,005 ___	131,210,335 ___	131,212,333 ___	131,210,302 ___
311,121,321 ___	313,213,213 ___	302,101,302 ___	132,012,135 ___

Name: _____   Date: _____

NCTM Standard: Number and Operations – understand the place-value structure of the base ten system

UNIT 1

Roll in Tricky Place Value

5,662	749	5,803	4,949
2,050	6,303	2,302	6,150
4,980	5,623	6,123	5,702
2,562	5,099	561	5,493

Determine the number represented by each item below, and find the answer in the boxes above. Write the item number on the line in the box that has the correct answer.

1. 56 tens, 20 hundreds, 2 ones
2. 56 hundreds, 3 ones, 2 tens
3. 6 tens, 56 hundreds, 2 ones
4. 56 hundreds, 20 tens, 3 ones
5. 20 tens, 61 ones, 3 hundreds
6. 20 tens, 61 hundreds, 3 ones
7. 61 hundreds, 20 ones, 3 tens
8. 61 hundreds, 3 ones, 2 tens
9. 20 hundreds, 3 tens, 20 ones
10. 50 tens, 2 hundreds, 49 ones
11. 49 tens, 50 hundreds, 3 ones
12. 49 hundreds, 3 tens, 50 ones
13. 49 ones, 0 tens, 49 hundreds
14. 49 ones, 5 tens, 50 hundreds
15. 20 hundreds, 30 tens, 2 ones
16. 40 tens, 53 hundreds, 2 ones

Name: _____ Date: _____

NCTM Standard: Number and Operations – understand the place-value structure of the base ten system

Wangle Some Big Whole Numbers

‾‾‾	‾‾‾	‾‾‾	‾‾‾
88,211	**99,921**	**52,211**	**98,710**
‾‾‾	‾‾‾	‾‾‾	‾‾‾
99,871	**65,310**	**21,110**	**85,310**
‾‾‾	‾‾‾	‾‾‾	‾‾‾
99,870	**93,210**	**98,210**	**10,000**
‾‾‾	‾‾‾	‾‾‾	‾‾‾
82,100	**21,100**	**83,210**	**22,110**

Rearrange the numbers in each item below to make the greatest number possible. Find that number in the boxes above. Write the item number on the line in the box that has the correct answer.

1.	5	6	0	3	1	**2.**	7	8	9	9	0
3.	1	0	8	3	2	**4.**	8	1	0	2	9
5.	9	2	1	9	9	**6.**	1	0	8	5	3
7.	0	1	0	2	8	**8.**	2	8	8	1	1
9.	8	7	9	1	0	**10.**	9	1	0	2	3
11.	1	2	0	1	2	**12.**	0	2	1	1	1
13.	0	0	0	1	0	**14.**	0	0	1	2	1
15.	7	8	9	9	1	**16.**	2	5	1	1	2

Name: _____ Date: _____

NCTM Standard: Number and Operations – compute fluently

Chalk Up a Sum

0 ___	7 ___	14 ___	3 ___
12 ___	4 ___	9 ___	1 ___
5 ___	8 ___	20 ___	6 ___
2 ___	13 ___	15 ___	10 ___

Find the answers to the following problems in the boxes above. Write the item number on the line in the box that has the correct answer.

1. 2 + 2 =

2. 0 + 0 =

3. 2 + 3 =

4. 3 + 3 =

5. 2 + 1 =

6. 5 + 5 =

7. 1 + 0 =

8. 1 + 1 =

9. 3 + 4 =

10. 4 + 4 =

11. 8 + 1 =

12. 10 + 2 =

13. 12 + 1 =

14. 13 + 1 =

15. 14 + 1 =

16. 10 + 10 =

UNIT 2

Name: _____ Date: _____

NCTM Standard: Number and Operations – compute fluently and make reasonable estimates

UNIT 2

Catch the Sum

75 __	70 __	65 __	55 __
100 __	40 __	45 __	110 __
60 __	15 __	50 __	160 __
125 __	80 __	25 __	95 __
85 __	180 __	90 __	120 __

Find the answers to the following problems in the boxes above. Write the item number on the line in the box that has the correct answer.

1. 10 + 30 =   **2.** 20 + 30 =   **3.** 30 + 50 =

4. 35 + 40 =   **5.** 45 + 50 =   **6.** 25 + 35 =

7. 45 + 45 =   **8.** 25 + 20 =   **9.** 35 + 20 =

10. 65 + 20 =   **11.** 35 + 30 =   **12.** 15 + 10 =

13. 20 + 50 =   **14.** 5 + 10 =   **15.** 40 + 60 =

16. 40 + 70 =   **17.** 50 + 75 =   **18.** 60 + 60 =

19. 90 + 90 =   **20.** 80 + 80 =

Name: _____ Date: _____

NCTM Standard: Number and Operations – understand relationships among numbers

UNIT 2

Grabbing *More Than* and *Less Than* Answers

3 ___	1 ___	11 ___	2 ___
16 ___	13 ___	17 ___	5 ___
6 ___	14 ___	12 ___	7 ___
10 ___	4 ___	18 ___	9 ___

Write the item number on the line in the box that has the correct answer. Find the number in the boxes above that is:

1. 5 more than 6   **2.** 4 more than 8   **3.** 4 more than 6

4. 6 more than 3   **5.** 3 more than 10   **6.** 3 less than 5

7. 3 less than 9   **8.** 5 less than 10   **9.** 6 less than 7

10. 5 less than 8   **11.** 6 less than 10   **12.** 5 less than 12

13. 4 less than 20   **14.** 5 less than 22   **15.** 6 less than 20

16. 5 less than 23

Name: _____ Date: _____

NCTM Standard: Number and Operations – compute fluently and make reasonable estimates

Drag in Addition Estimation

15,000 ___	9,000 ___	6,000 ___
13,000 ___	18,000 ___	8,000 ___
16,000 ___	12,000 ___	10,000 ___
5,000 ___	11,000 ___	4,000 ___
14,000 ___	19,000 ___	7,000 ___

Round the numbers in each problem below to the nearest thousands, add, and then find the answer in the boxes above. Write the item number on the line in the box that has the correct answer.

1. 3,458 + 9,432 =   2. 4,562 + 7,811 =
3. 5,678 + 2,132 =   4. 2,315 + 2,564 =
5. 5,672 + 1,256 =   6. 7,501 + 2,341 =
7. 4,579 + 3,910 =   8. 2,199 + 2,446 =
9. 4,256 + 7,199 =   10. 6,100 + 8,256 =
11. 5,298 + 1,459 =   12. 7,890 + 8,154 =
13. 7,190 + 8,499 =   14. 9,199 + 9,988 =
15. 8,900 + 9,199 =

Name: _____   Date: _____

NCTM Standard: Number and Operations – compute fluently and make reasonable estimates

UNIT 2

Rope Some Averages

300 ___	600 ___	60 ___	90 ___
400 ___	30 ___	70 ___	40 ___
700 ___	80 ___	20 ___	500 ___
100 ___	50 ___	1,000 ___	200 ___

Round each number below to the largest place value, and then find their sum's approximate average in the boxes above. Write the item number on the line in the box that has the correct answer.

1. 13 + 42 + 36 =

2. 56 + 22 + 97 =

3. 21 + 24 + 23 =

4. 728 + 678 + 690 + 710 =

5. 202 + 200 + 202 =

6. 260 + 250 + 325 =

7. 540 + 510 + 210 =

8. 25 + 34 + 69 + 29 =

9. 39 + 79 + 58 + 21 =

10. 97 + 98 + 99 + 95 =

11. 45 + 68 + 91 + 71 =

12. 95 + 81 + 92 + 91 =

13. 79 + 82 + 81 + 78 =

14. 510 + 529 + 498 + 476 =

15. 985 + 1,463 + 990 =

16. 590 + 649 + 629 + 597 =

Name: _____ Date: _____

NCTM Standard: Number and Operations – identify and use relationships between operations, such as subtraction as the inverse of addition, to solve problems

Rescue Inverse Operations

147 - 62	101 - 39	130 - 74	153 - 64
___	___	___	___
117 - 45	59 - 27	140 - 75	73 - 17
___	___	___	___
127 - 75	139 - 62	115 - 73	135 - 72
___	___	___	___
80 - 23	104 - 32	90 - 45	108 - 54
___	___	___	___

Find the inverse operation of each problem below in the boxes above. Write the item number on the line in the box that has the correct answer.

1. $56 + 74 =$ **2.** $27 + 32 =$ **3.** $52 + 75 =$

4. $45 + 45 =$ **5.** $63 + 72 =$ **6.** $57 + 23 =$

7. $85 + 62 =$ **8.** $65 + 75 =$ **9.** $77 + 62 =$

10. $89 + 64 =$ **11.** $72 + 45 =$ **12.** $72 + 32 =$

13. $62 + 39 =$ **14.** $42 + 73 =$ **15.** $54 + 54 =$

16. $56 + 17 =$

Name: _____   Date: _____

NCTM Standard: Number and Operations – compute fluently

Claim a Difference

7 ___	4 ___	8 ___
12 ___	10 ___	2 ___
3 ___	9 ___	15 ___
5 ___	11 ___	6 ___
1 ___	13 ___	14 ___

Solve each problem below, and find the answer in the boxes above. Write the item number on the line in the box that has the correct answer.

1. $15 - 5 =$

2. $13 - 7 =$

3. $12 - 7 =$

4. $17 - 8 =$

5. $13 - 6 =$

6. $15 - 3 =$

7. $14 - 6 =$

8. $15 - 2 =$

9. $18 - 7 =$

10. $17 - 3 =$

11. $17 - 2 =$

12. $14 - 11 =$

13. $15 - 14 =$

14. $16 - 12 =$

15. $13 - 11 =$

Name: _____ Date: _____

NCTM Standard: Number and Operations – compute fluently

Gain a Difference

34 ___	**9** ___	**44** ___	**5** ___
23 ___	**22** ___	**33** ___	**25** ___
37 ___	**18** ___	**15** ___	**2** ___
12 ___	**26** ___	**30** ___	**41** ___

Solve each problem below, and find the answer in the boxes above. Write the item number on the line in the box that has the correct answer.

1. 14 - 9 =

2. 27 - 5 =

3. 35 - 5 =

4. 46 - 12 =

5. 14 - 5 =

6. 14 - 2 =

7. 27 - 12 =

8. 46 - 5 =

9. 14 - 12 =

10. 46 - 9 =

11. 35 - 9 =

12. 46 - 2 =

13. 27 - 9 =

14. 35 - 12 =

15. 27 - 2 =

16. 35 - 2 =

Name: _____ Date: _____

NCTM Standard: Number and Operations – compute fluently and make reasonable estimates

Peg Subtraction Answers

159	2,121	296	1,457
___	___	___	___
775	36	317	811
___	___	___	___
851	235	390	2,062
___	___	___	___
511	591	642	850
___	___	___	___

Using mental math only, choose the answer for each subtraction problem from the boxes above. Write the item number on the line in the box that has the correct answer.

1. 394 - 235 =
2. 756 - 521 =
3. 984 - 342 =
4. 1,238 - 921 =
5. 2,721 - 659 =
6. 742 - 231 =
7. 896 - 121 =
8. 2,548 - 1,091 =
9. 2,245 - 124 =
10. 521 - 131 =
11. 982 - 131 =
12. 942 - 131 =
13. 134 - 98 =
14. 385 - 89 =
15. 879 - 29 =
16. 780 - 189 =

Name: _____   Date: _____

NCTM Standard: Number and Operations – compute fluently

Score With Multiples of 3 and 4

For each problem below, find the answer in the boxes to the right. Write the item number on the line in the box that has the correct answer.

44 __	**6** __	**24** __	**28** __
9 __	**33** __	**48** __	**15** __
40 __	**21** __	**20** __	**39** __
12 __	**36** __	**18** __	**8** __
32 __	**30** __	**27** __	**16** __

1. 3 x 3 =

2. 3 x 6 =

3. 4 x 3 =

4. 5 x 3 =

5. 7 x 3 =

6. 8 x 3 =

7. 2 x 3 =

8. 3 x 9 =

9. 10 x 3 =

10. 11 x 3 =

11. 3 x 13 =

12. 2 x 4 =

13. 4 x 9 =

14. 4 x 5 =

15. 7 x 4 =

16. 10 x 4 =

17. 8 x 4 =

18. 11 x 4 =

19. 4 x 4 =

20. 12 x 4 =

Name: _____ Date: _____

NCTM Standard: Number and Operations – compute fluently

Nab Multiples of 5 and 6

For each problem below, find the answer in the boxes to the right. Write the item number on the line in the box that has the correct answer.

1. 6 x 2 =	
2. 7 x 6 =	
3. 6 x 3 =	
4. 6 x 4 =	
5. 5 x 2 =	
6. 4 x 5 =	
7. 5 x 5 =	
8. 6 x 6 =	
9. 5 x 9 =	
10. 12 x 6 =	
11. 8 x 5 =	
12. 10 x 5 =	
13. 10 x 6 =	
14. 6 x 5 =	
15. 5 x 3 =	
16. 6 x 8 =	
17. 5 x 11 =	
18. 6 x 11 =	
19. 9 x 6 =	
20. 7 x 5 =	

12 __	48 __	72 __	60 __
66 __	20 __	36 __	54 __
18 __	40 __	55 __	42 __
15 __	25 __	45 __	35 __
30 __	50 __	10 __	24 __

Name: _____ Date: _____

NCTM Standard: Number and Operations – compute fluently

Conquer Big Multiples

4,900	1,600	2,000	4,200
2,400	3,200	1,200	9,000
1,000	2,800	7,200	4,500
3,000	600	1,500	6,400
800	1,800	4,800	2,500

For each problem below, find the answer in the boxes above. Write the item number on the line in the box that has the correct answer.

1. 20 x 40 =   2. 30 x 20 =   3. 50 x 20 =

4. 20 x 60 =   5. 30 x 50 =   6. 40 x 50 =

7. 40 x 60 =   8. 50 x 90 =   9. 30 x 60 =

10. 40 x 40 =   11. 40 x 70 =   12. 40 x 80 =

13. 50 x 50 =   14. 50 x 60 =   15. 60 x 70 =

16. 60 x 80 =   17. 70 x 70 =   18. 80 x 90 =

19. 80 x 80 =   20. 90 x 100 =

Name: _____ Date: _____

NCTM Standard: Number and Operations – compute fluently

UNIT 3

Snag a Big Multiple

___ **1,800**	___ **1,600**	___ **2,700**	___ **1,500**
___ **1,200**	___ **1,000**	___ **800**	___ **3,200**
___ **6,300**	___ **3,500**	___ **2,500**	___ **4,900**
___ **2,100**	___ **3,000**	___ **4,800**	___ **400**

Round each factor to the nearest ten and then multiply. Find the answer in the boxes above. Write the item number on the line in the box that has the correct answer.

1. 23 x 35 =   **2.** 25 x 62 =   **3.** 67 x 32 =

4. 75 x 21 =   **5.** 78 x 42 =   **6.** 85 x 25 =

7. 92 x 67 =   **8.** 52 x 28 =   **9.** 53 x 61 =

10. 65 x 74 =   **11.** 68 x 51 =   **12.** 98 x 12 =

13. 63 x 79 =   **14.** 24 x 23 =   **15.** 25 x 38 =

16. 45 x 52 =

Name: _____ Date: _____

NCTM Standard: Number and Operations – identify and use relationships between operations, such as division as the inverse of multiplication

Grasp the Inverse Operation

___	___	___	___
162 ÷ 2 =	124 ÷ 2 =	168 ÷ 3 =	72 ÷ 6 =
___	___	___	___
126 ÷ 6 =	126 ÷ 3 =	208 ÷ 4 =	144 ÷ 6 =
___	___	___	___
184 ÷ 2 =	156 ÷ 3 =	125 ÷ 5 =	216 ÷ 3 =
___	___	___	___
99 ÷ 3 =	46 ÷ 2 =	75 ÷ 5 =	186 ÷ 3 =

For each of the problems below, find the corresponding inverse operation in the boxes above. Write the item number on the line in the box that has the correct answer.

1. 24 x 6 =   **2.** 56 x 3 =   **3.** 33 x 3 =

4. 42 x 3 =   **5.** 12 x 6 =   **6.** 15 x 5 =

7. 25 x 5 =   **8.** 62 x 2 =   **9.** 52 x 3 =

10. 72 x 3 =   **11.** 81 x 2 =   **12.** 92 x 2 =

13. 21 x 6 =   **14.** 23 x 2 =   **15.** 52 x 4 =

16. 62 x 3 =

Name: _____ Date: _____

NCTM Standard: Number and Operations – identify and use relationships between operations, such as multiplication as the inverse of division

Haul in Some Inverse Operations

____ 90 x 9 =	____ 7 x 30 =	____ 50 x 5 =	____ 70 x 6 =
____ 40 x 6 =	____ 80 x 7 =	____ 90 x 8 =	____ 6 x 50 =
____ 3 x 90 =	____ 70 x 4 =	____ 90 x 7 =	____ 5 x 90 =
____ 9 x 60 =	____ 50 x 7 =	____ 4 x 90 =	____ 8 x 60 =

For each of the problems below, find the corresponding inverse operation in the boxes above. Write the item number on the line in the box that has the correct answer.

1. 560 ÷ 7 =	**2.** 250 ÷ 5 =	**3.** 240 ÷ 6 =
4. 280 ÷ 4 =	**5.** 630 ÷ 7 =	**6.** 720 ÷ 8 =
7. 810 ÷ 9 =	**8.** 300 ÷ 6 =	**9.** 420 ÷ 6 =
10. 480 ÷ 8 =	**11.** 540 ÷ 9 =	**12.** 210 ÷ 7 =
13. 270 ÷ 3 =	**14.** 350 ÷ 7 =	**15.** 360 ÷ 4 =
16. 450 ÷ 5 =		

Name: _____   Date: _____

NCTM Standard: Number and Operations – compute fluently and make reasonable estimates

Charge for the Quotient

$7\frac{3}{4}$ ___	$1\frac{1}{4}$ ___	$5\frac{1}{3}$ ___	$8\frac{3}{8}$ ___
$6\frac{1}{4}$ ___	$8\frac{1}{6}$ ___	$2\frac{7}{9}$ ___	$3\frac{2}{5}$ ___
$7\frac{7}{8}$ ___	$7\frac{1}{2}$ ___	$9\frac{8}{9}$ ___	$9\frac{2}{5}$ ___
$3\frac{2}{7}$ ___	$4\frac{1}{9}$ ___	$7\frac{3}{8}$ ___	$3\frac{1}{3}$ ___

Solve the problems below, and find the answers in the boxes above. Reduce fractions to lowest terms. Write the item number on the line in the box that has the correct answer.

1. $15 \div 12 =$ 2. $25 \div 4 =$ 3. $15 \div 2 =$

4. $23 \div 7 =$ 5. $32 \div 6 =$ 6. $40 \div 12 =$

7. $31 \div 4 =$ 8. $17 \div 5 =$ 9. $59 \div 8 =$

10. $49 \div 6 =$ 11. $47 \div 5 =$ 12. $63 \div 8 =$

13. $25 \div 9 =$ 14. $37 \div 9 =$ 15. $67 \div 8 =$

16. $89 \div 9 =$

Name: _____   Date: _____

NCTM Standard: Number and Operations – compute fluently and make reasonable estimates

A Quotient Sprint

200 ___	**10** ___	$3\frac{1}{6}$ ___	$11\frac{4}{5}$ ___
$4\frac{3}{4}$ ___	$10\frac{5}{9}$ ___	**19** ___	**40** ___
100 ___	$9\frac{1}{2}$ ___	$47\frac{1}{2}$ ___	$6\frac{1}{3}$ ___
15 ___	**59** ___	**20** ___	**2** ___

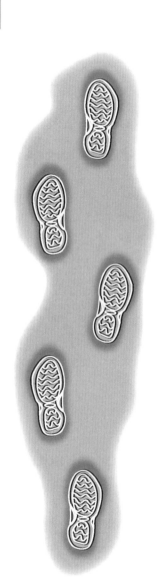

Find the answers to the following problems in the boxes above. Write the item number on the line in the box that has the correct answer.

1. $95 \div 9 =$ 2. $475 \div 10 =$

3. $590 \div 10 =$ 4. $1{,}000 \div 5 =$

5. $750 \div 375 =$ 6. $1{,}000 \div 25 =$

7. $475 \div 50 =$ 8. $95 \div 30 =$

9. $95 \div 15 =$ 10. $475 \div 100 =$

11. $750 \div 50 =$ 12. $590 \div 50 =$

13. $750 \div 75 =$ 14. $475 \div 25 =$

15. $1{,}000 \div 50 =$ 16. $1{,}000 \div 10 =$

Name: _____ Date: _____

NCTM Standard: Number and Operations – compute fluently and make reasonable estimates

Cart Off Some Quotients

0.2 ___	**15** ___	**2.5** ___	**0.05** ___
0.8 ___	**4** ___	**1.6** ___	**30** ___
1 ___	**10** ___	**3** ___	**1.25** ___
45 ___	**0.09** ___	**2** ___	**0.08** ___

Round the dividend (the first number) to the greatest place value and divide, and then find the answer to each problem in the boxes above. Write the item number on the line in the box that has the correct answer.

1. 0.45 ÷ 10 =
2. 6.5 ÷ 7 =
3. 8.6 ÷ 3 =
4. 0.89 ÷ 10 =
5. 0.36 ÷ 5 =
6. 0.95 ÷ 5 =
7. 5.6 ÷ 3 =
8. 3.6 ÷ 5 =
9. 0.75 ÷ 0.5 =
10. 5.7 ÷ 0.2 =
11. 7.8 ÷ 2 =
12. 9.2 ÷ 0.2 =
13. 4.7 ÷ 2 =
14. 4.8 ÷ 4 =
15. 5.9 ÷ 0.6 =
16. 5.8 ÷ 0.4 =

Name: _____ Date: _____

NCTM Standard: Number and Operations – compute fluently and make reasonable estimates

Grapple for Some Quotients

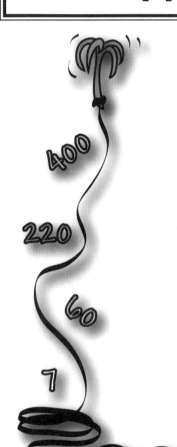

400 ___	220 ___	100 ___	10 ___
110 ___	70 ___	90 ___	40 ___
240 ___	130 ___	20 ___	80 ___
50 ___	7 ___	120 ___	60 ___

Round the dividend (the first number) to a compatible number and divide, and then find the answer to each problem in the boxes above. Write the item number on the line in the box that has the correct answer.

1. $542 \div 6 =$

2. $637 \div 8 =$

3. $492 \div 7 =$

4. $428 \div 60 =$

5. $809 \div 2 =$

6. $242 \div 4 =$

7. $328 \div 8 =$

8. $263 \div 2 =$

9. $719 \div 7 =$

10. $551 \div 5 =$

11. $359 \div 3 =$

12. $443 \div 2 =$

13. $298 \div 6 =$

14. $182 \div 9 =$

15. $484 \div 2 =$

16. $218 \div 20 =$

Name: _____ Date: _____

NCTM Standard: Number and Operations – compute fluently and make reasonable estimates

Dive Into Challenging Division

___ 400	___ 80	___ 200	___ 66
___ 90	___ 900	___ 30	___ 500
___ 1,000	___ 600	___ 20	___ 800
___ 5,000	___ 700	___ 3,000	___ 300

Estimate the following problems by rounding the dividend to a compatible number. Find the answer in the boxes above. Write the item number on the line in the box that has the correct answer.

1. 27,302 ÷ 90   =   2. 27,100 ÷ 70   =
3. 75,200 ÷ 75   =   4. 73,102 ÷ 80   =
5. 84,900 ÷ 110 =   6. 62,899 ÷ 700 =
7. 49,798 ÷ 10   =   8. 36,101 ÷ 1,200 =
9. 24,897 ÷ 50   =   10. 29,099 ÷ 10   =
11. 72,123 ÷ 900 =   12. 66,213 ÷ 1,000 =
13. 31,978 ÷ 50   =   14. 41,870 ÷ 60   =
15. 17,999 ÷ 90   =   16. 18,101 ÷ 900 =

Name: _____ Date: _____

NCTM Standard: Number and Operations – compute fluently

Decimal Dash

0.0056 ___	0.015 ___	0.032 ___
0.028 ___	0.024 ___	0.0035 ___
0.0040 ___	0.28 ___	0.020 ___
0.21 ___	0.049 ___	0.035 ___
0.056 ___	0.12 ___	0.021 ___

Solve each of the problems below, and then find the answer in the boxes above. Write the item number on the line in the box that has the correct answer.

1. 0.4 x 0.7 =   **2.** 0.4 x 0.3 =   **3.** 0.4 x 0.05 =

4. 0.4 x 0.07 =   **5.** 0.4 x 0.08 =   **6.** 0.05 x 0.07 =

7. 0.05 x 0.08 =   **8.** 0.07 x 0.08 =   **9.** 0.3 x 0.05 =

10. 0.3 x 0.07 =   **11.** 0.3 x 0.08 =   **12.** 0.7 x 0.3 =

13. 0.7 x 0.05 =   **14.** 0.7 x 0.07 =   **15.** 0.7 x 0.08 =

Name: _____ Date: _____

NCTM Standard: Number and Operations – understand ways of representing numbers and work flexibly with fractions, decimals, and percents

Drag in Decimals on a Number Line

16.5 ___	0.16 ___	12.5 ___
0.11 ___	0.13 ___	1.5 ___
5.5 ___	10.75 ___	20.25 ___
0.12 ___	2.25 ___	0.25 ___
15.25 ___	20.75 ___	0.15 ___

Determine the decimal that would be at the arrow on each number line below. Find the decimal represented by the arrow in the boxes above. Write the item number on the line in the box that has the correct answer.

1. 1 ⬆ 2	**2.** 2 ⬆ 3
3. 5 ⬆ 6	**4.** 10 ⬆ 11
5. 15 ⬆ 16	**6.** 16 ⬆ 17
7. 0.10 ⬆ 0.20	**8.** 0.10 ⬆ 0.14
9. 20 ⬆ 21	**10.** 0.20 ⬆ 0.30
11. 20 ⬆ 21	**12.** 0.15 ⬆ 0.17
13. 0.10 ⬆ 0.12	**14.** 0.12 ⬆ 0.14
15. 12 ⬆ 14	

Name: _____ Date: _____

NCTM Standard: Number and Operations – compute fluently and make reasonable estimates

UNIT 4

Nab a Product

—	—	—	—
108.9	50.5	4.5	28
—	—	—	—
50.4	2.5	254.1	60.5
—	—	—	—
151.5	10.5	181.5	117.6
—	—	—	—
7.5	84	212.1	90.9

Find the answers to the following problems in the boxes above. Write the item number on the line in the box that has the correct answer.

1. 0.5 x 101 =   **2.** 2.1 x 101 =   **3.** 0.9 x 56 =

4. 2.1 x 121 =   **5.** 1.5 x 5 =   **6.** 0.9 x 121 =

7. 0.5 x 56 =   **8.** 0.9 x 5 =   **9.** 2.1 x 56 =

10. 1.5 x 101 =   **11.** 1.5 x 121 =   **12.** 2.1 x 5 =

13. 0.9 x 101 =   **14.** 1.5 x 56 =   **15.** 0.5 x 5 =

16. 0.5 x 121 =

Name: _____ Date: _____

NCTM Standard: Number and Operations – compute fluently

Snare Decimal Multiples

___ 0.006	___ 0.81	___ 0.20	___ 0.025
___ 0.035	___ 0.028	___ 0.064	___ 0.032
___ 0.036	___ 0.021	___ 0.01	___ 0.16
___ 0.018	___ 0.18	___ 0.049	___ 0.30

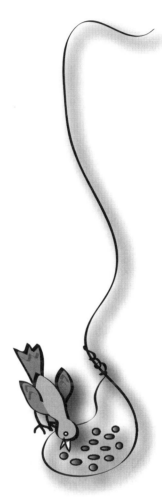

Find the answers to the following problems in the boxes above. Write the item number on the line in the box that has the correct answer.

1. 0.02 x 0.3 =

2. 0.4 x 0.5 =

3. 0.07 x 0.3 =

4. 0.4 x 0.4 =

5. 0.6 x 0.5 =

6. 0.08 x 0.8 =

7. 0.9 x 0.9 =

8. 0.07 x 0.4 =

9. 0.6 x 0.03 =

10. 0.6 x 0.3 =

11. 0.5 x 0.05 =

12. 0.4 x 0.08 =

13. 0.07 x 0.7 =

14. 0.4 x 0.09 =

15. 0.05 x 0.7 =

16. 0.1 x 0.1 =

Name: _____ Date: _____

NCTM Standard: Number and Operations – compute fluently and make reasonable estimates

Snap Up Change

___ $8.75	___ $3.75	___ $9.25	___ $9.70
___ $17.75	___ $8.90	___ $14.65	___ $14.40
___ $4.00	___ $4.75	___ $17.90	___ $13.75
___ $14.75	___ $13.65	___ $13.15	___ $15.75

If you had a twenty-dollar bill and you spent the following amounts, find the amount of change you would receive from the clerk in the boxes above. Write the item number on the line in the box that has the correct answer.

1. $5 $5 $1 10¢   2. $1 $1 5¢ 5¢   3. $5 25¢

4. $5 $5 25¢ 25¢ 25¢   5. $1 $1 $1 $1 25¢

6. $5 $1 $5 25¢   7. $5 $5 $5 $1

8. 10¢ 10¢ 10¢ 10¢ 10¢ 10¢ $5

9. $5 $1 25¢ 10¢   10. 10¢ 10¢ 10¢ $5 $5

11. $1 $5 5¢ 5¢ 5¢ 5¢ 5¢   12. $1 $5 25¢ $5 $5

13. $1 25¢ 25¢ 25¢ 10¢ $5   14. $5 $5 $5 25¢

15. $1 $1 25¢   16. $5 5¢ 5¢ 5¢ 5¢ 5¢ 5¢ 5¢

Name: _____   Date: _____

NCTM Standard: Number and Operations – understand the place-value structure of the base ten system

Earn Some Decimals

13.033 ___	36.36 ___	2.0032 ___	13.003 ___
2.306 ___	13.030 ___	3.036 ___	2.0003 ___
3.0036 ___	3.013 ___	13.0003 ___	30.306 ___
3.0306 ___	2.0306 ___	2.032 ___	3.0030 ___

The decimals are written in word form below. Find the matching decimals written in numerical form in the boxes above. Write the item number on the line in the box that has the correct answer.

1. three and thirty-six ten thousandths
2. three and thirty-six thousandths
3. three and three hundred six ten thousandths
4. thirty-six and thirty-six hundredths
5. three and thirty ten thousandths
6. three and thirteen thousandths
7. thirteen and thirty thousandths
8. thirteen and three thousandths
9. thirteen and three ten thousandths
10. thirty and three hundred six thousandths
11. two and three hundred six ten thousandths
12. two and three hundred six thousandths
13. two and three ten thousandths
14. two and thirty-two thousandths
15. two and thirty-two ten thousandths
16. thirteen and thirty-three thousandths

BONUS!
2.0306

Pay to the Order of:
$ 13.030

Name: _____ Date: _____

NCTM Standard: Number and Operations – understand the place-value structure of the base ten system

Get Ready to Nab Decimals on a Number Line

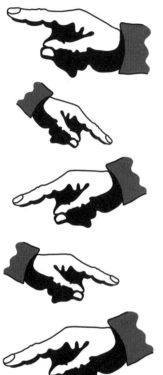

0.265 ___	**0.2555** ___	**0.261** ___
0.2575 ___	**0.256** ___	**0.270** ___
0.2565 ___	**0.262** ___	**0.259** ___
0.257 ___	**0.2560** ___	**0.2551** ___
0.2553 ___	**0.280** ___	**0.264** ___

Determine the decimal that would be at the location of the arrow, and then find the answer in the boxes above. Write the item number on the line in the box that has the correct answer.

1. 0.255 ↑ 0.257   2. 0.255 ↑ 0.259

3. 0.260 ↑ 0.262   4. 0.260 ↑ 0.268

5. 0.258 ↑ 0.260   6. 0.2550 ↑ 0.2556

7. 0.2550 ↑ 0.2560   8. 0.2550 ↑ 0.2570

9. 0.2550 ↑ 0.2580   10. 0.2550 ↑ 0.2552

11. 0.260 ↑ 0.264   12. 0.260 ↑ 0.300

13. 0.260 ↑ 0.280   14. 0.260 ↑ 0.270

15. 0.2550 ↑ 0.2600

Name: _____ Date: _____

NCTM Standard: Number and Operations – understand numbers and ways of representing numbers

Swoop Up Rounding Decimals

0.3 ___	1.2 ___	0.1 ___
2.7 ___	0.0 ___	0.4 ___
0.7 ___	3.0 ___	4.7 ___
1.0 ___	2.0 ___	0.9 ___
0.2 ___	0.8 ___	1.8 ___

Round the following numbers to the tenths place. Then find the answers in the boxes above. Write the item number on the line in the box that has the correct answer.

1. 1.23	**2.** 0.39	**3.** 0.658
4. 0.798	**5.** 0.3421	**6.** 0.21
7. 1.79	**8.** 2.71	**9.** 0.8944
10. 0.95	**11.** 4.7211	**12.** 0.015
13. 0.0982	**14.** 1.999	**15.** 3.0127

Name: _____   Date: _____

NCTM Standard: Number and Operations – understand numbers and ways of representing numbers

UNIT 4

Reap Rounding Decimals to the Hundredths

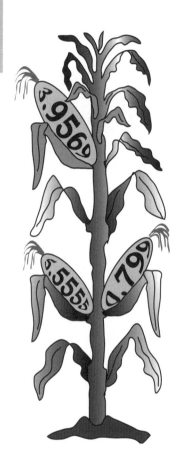

2.79 ___	1.01 ___	5.56 ___
0.03 ___	1.57 ___	3.96 ___
7.00 ___	0.01 ___	0.31 ___
0.80 ___	9.00 ___	0.12 ___
4.01 ___	0.11 ___	3.00 ___

Round the following decimals to the hundredths place, and then find the answer in the boxes above. Write the item number on the line in the box that has the correct answer.

1.	1.568		**2.**	2.791		**3.**	0.1222
4.	0.799		**5.**	3.001		**6.**	4.008
7.	5.5555		**8.**	7.0001		**9.**	0.105
10.	0.309		**11.**	8.999		**12.**	0.005
13.	1.011		**14.**	0.029		**15.**	3.9569

Name: _____ Date: _____

NCTM Standard: Number and Operations – understand numbers and ways of representing numbers

Rack Up Rounding Decimals to the Thousandths

0.401 ___	2.043 ___	3.000 ___
6.013 ___	1.089 ___	0.900 ___
1.000 ___	1.900 ___	2.981 ___
6.012 ___	0.400 ___	0.111 ___
0.112 ___	0.901 ___	0.113 ___

Round the decimals below to the thousandths place, and find the answer in the boxes above. Write the item number on the line in the box that has the correct answer.

1. 0.40056	**2.** 0.9009	**3.** 1.0001
4. 2.9812	**5.** 6.0115	**6.** 0.1123
7. 1.0892	**8.** 2.0433	**9.** 6.0129
10. 0.4001	**11.** 1.8999	**12.** 0.9000
13. 0.1127	**14.** 2.9999	**15.** 0.1111

Name: _____   Date: _____

NCTM Standard: Number and Operations – understand the place-value structure of the base ten system

UNIT 4

Sweep Up Decimals

Determine the decimal numeral represented by the dots in each place below, and find the matching number in the boxes below. Write the item number on the line in the box that has the correct answer.

●	tenths	hundredths	thousandths	ten thousandths
1.	•••••	••••• •	••••• ••	••••• ••••
2.	••••	••••• •	•••••	••••
3.	•••••	••••	••••• •••	••••• •••
4.	••••	••••• •	••••	••••• ••••
5.	•••••	••••• •	••••• ••	••••• •••
6.	•••••	••••• ••••	•••••	••••
7.	••••	••••• ••	••••	••••• •••
8.	•••••	••••• •	••••• •	••••• ••••
9.	••••	••••• •	••••• ••••	••••• ••••
10.	••••• •••		••••• ••••	••••• ••••
11.	••••• •••	•	••••• ••••	••••• •••
12.	••••• •••	••••• ••••	••••• ••••	••••• ••••

___	___	___	___	___	___
0.4699	**0.5679**	**0.5954**	**0.5488**	**0.4748**	**0.8198**

___	___	___	___	___	___
0.8099	**0.4649**	**0.8999**	**0.5669**	**0.4654**	**0.5678**

Name: _____   Date: _____

NCTM Standard: Number and Operations – understand the place-value structure of the base ten system

Tag Some Ordered Decimals

‾‾ 0.25, 0.33, 0.35	‾‾ 0.04, 0.05, 0.40	‾‾ 0.04, 0.39, 0.4
‾‾ 0.05, 0.29, 0.50	‾‾ 0.24, 0.29, 0.42	‾‾ 0.03, 0.34, 0.53
‾‾ 0.03, 0.3, 0.33	‾‾ 0.39, 0.90, 0.92	‾‾ 0.34, 0.42, 0.43
‾‾ 0.03, 0.29, 0.30	‾‾ 0.3, 0.32, 0.33	‾‾ 0.05, 0.38, 0.39
‾‾ 0.29, 0.33, 0.34	‾‾ 0.39, 0.4, 0.42	‾‾ 0.03, 0.33, 0.35

Place the following sets of decimals in order from least to greatest, and find the answers in the boxes above. Write the item number on the line in the box that has the correct answer.

1. 0.03, 0.33, 0.3
2. 0.33, 0.35, 0.03
3. 0.33, 0.3, 0.32
4. 0.34, 0.53, 0.03
5. 0.35, 0.25, 0.33
6. 0.34, 0.33, 0.29
7. 0.34, 0.43, 0.42
8. 0.42, 0.24, 0.29
9. 0.42, 0.39, 0.4
10. 0.4, 0.39, 0.04
11. 0.03, 0.30, 0.29
12. 0.04, 0.40, 0.05
13. 0.05, 0.38, 0.39
14. 0.05, 0.50, 0.29
15. 0.39, 0.92, 0.90

Name: _____ Date: _____

NCTM Standard: Number and Operations – compute fluently; make reasonable estimates; understand the base ten system

Ambush Some Decimal Round-ups

0.64 ___	0.24 ___	0.63 ___	0.10 ___
0.30 ___	0.16 ___	0.15 ___	0.40 ___
0.42 ___	0.45 ___	0.27 ___	0.54 ___
0.20 ___	0.72 ___	0.18 ___	0.12 ___

Round all the decimals below to the tenths place, and then estimate the answers. Find the correct answers in the boxes above. Write the item number on the line in the box that has the correct answer.

1. $0.567 \times 0.432 =$
2. $0.55 \times 0.67 =$
3. $0.312 \times 0.521 =$
4. $0.34 \times 0.56 =$
5. $0.567 \times 0.89 =$
6. $0.421 \times 0.544 =$
7. $0.598 \times 0.522 =$
8. $0.943 \times 0.45 =$
9. $0.192 \times 0.542 =$
10. $0.24 \times 0.567 =$
11. $0.221 \times 0.841 =$
12. $0.78 \times 0.93 =$
13. $0.298 \times 0.943 =$
14. $0.798 \times 0.817 =$
15. $0.902 \times 0.724 =$
16. $0.54 \times 0.789 =$

Name: _____ Date: _____

NCTM Standard: Number and Operations – compute fluently; **Algebra** – use symbolic algebra to represent problems

Dive for Decimal Quotient Unknowns

300 ___	**900** ___	**4,000** ___
2,700 ___	**2,500** ___	**1,000** ___
2,000 ___	**500** ___	**400** ___
8,000 ___	**3,500** ___	**6,000** ___
3,000 ___	**5,000** ___	**600** ___

Solve the problems below by finding the unknown decimal quotients in each. Find the correct answers in the boxes above. Write the item number on the line in the box that has the correct answer.

1. $420 \div 0.7 = n$
2. $640 \div 0.08 = m$
3. $540 \div 0.6 = t$
4. $320 \div 0.8 = y$
5. $200 \div 0.2 = a$
6. $810 \div 0.3 = n$
7. $400 \div 0.8 = m$
8. $250 \div 0.05 = t$
9. $240 \div 0.12 = y$
10. $300 \div 0.05 = a$
11. $180 \div 0.6 = n$
12. $160 \div 0.04 = m$
13. $500 \div 0.2 = t$
14. $600 \div 0.2 = y$
15. $700 \div 0.2 = a$

Name: _____ Date: _____

NCTM Standard: Number and Operations – compute fluently and make reasonable estimates

Extract Some Decimal Division Estimates

between 20 & 30 ___	between 5 & 6 ___	between 2 & 3 ___
between 300 & 400 ___	between 11 & 12 ___	between 600 & 700 ___
between 13 & 14 ___	between 6 & 7 ___	between 0.3 & 0.4 ___
between 0.06 & 0.07 ___	between 0.5 & 0.6 ___	between 100 & 200 ___
between 500 & 600 ___	between 1 & 2 ___	between 0.02 & 0.03 ___

Estimate the division problems below, and find the matching range of the quotient for each in the boxes above. Write the item number on the line in the box that has the correct answer.

1. $59.65 \div 10 =$

2. $67.85 \div 0.20 =$

3. $67.85 \div 10 =$

4. $0.5789 \div 0.20 =$

5. $0.6785 \div 10 =$

6. $0.5965 \div 20 =$

7. $5.789 \div 10 =$

8. $6.785 \div 20 =$

9. $5,789 \div 10 =$

10. $69.65 \div 0.10 =$

11. $5.789 \div 0.20 =$

12. $57.89 \div 50 =$

13. $578.9 \div 50 =$

14. $6.785 \div 0.50 =$

15. $5,965 \div 50 =$

Name: _____ Date: _____

NCTM Standard: Number and Operations – compute fluently and make reasonable estimates

Groove With Decimal Multiples

280 ___	210 ___	60 ___
240 ___	150 ___	160 ___
66 ___	250 ___	720 ___
320 ___	200 ___	120 ___
180 ___	90 ___	270 ___

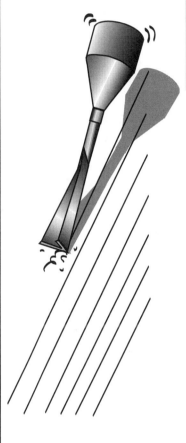

Try to mentally calculate the following problems, and then find the answers in the boxes above. Write the item number on the line in the box that has the correct answer.

1. 0.5 x 500 =   **2.** 0.2 x 300 =   **3.** 0.3 x 600 =

4. 0.3 x 220 =   **5.** 0.6 x 200 =   **6.** 0.7 x 300 =

7. 0.8 x 400 =   **8.** 0.9 x 800 =   **9.** 0.3 x 300 =

10. 0.4 x 400 =   **11.** 0.4 x 500 =   **12.** 0.5 x 300 =

13. 0.6 x 400 =   **14.** 0.7 x 400 =   **15.** 0.9 x 300 =

Name: _____ Date: _____

NCTM Standard: Number and Operations – understand relationships among numbers; use factors to solve problems

Factor Find

2, 3 4, 6	2, 3, 4, 6, 8, 12	2, 4, 8, 16, 32	2, 7
2, 4, 5, 10	2, 3, 6, 7, 14, 21	2, 4, 8, 16	3, 7
2, 5, 7, 10, 35	3, 5	2, 5	2, 3, 4, 6, 9, 18
2, 4	2, 13	3, 5 15, 25	3, 9, 27

For each of the following numbers, find its factors, excluding the number 1 and the number itself, in the boxes above. Write the item number on the line in the box that has the correct answer.

1. 12	**2.** 15	**3.** 32	**4.** 64
5. 70	**6.** 24	**7.** 81	**8.** 8
9. 10	**10.** 20	**11.** 14	**12.** 36
13. 26	**14.** 42	**15.** 21	**16.** 75

Name: _____ Date: _____

NCTM Standard: Number and Operations – identify and use relationships between operations, such as division as the inverse of multiplication, to solve problems

Grapple With
Greatest Common Factors (GCF)

9 ___	3 ___	12 ___	10 ___
6 ___	7 ___	5 ___	13 ___
11 ___	2 ___	20 ___	21 ___
1 ___	14 ___	15 ___	8 ___

Choose the greatest common factor (GCF) of each set of numbers below, and then find it in the boxes above. Write the item number on the line in the box that has the correct answer.

1. 14 and 12	**2.** 12 and 6	**3.** 15 and 20
4. 21 and 14	**5.** 32 and 15	**6.** 8 and 16
7. 9 and 21	**8.** 40 and 30	**9.** 18 and 27
10. 40 and 60	**11.** 42 and 63	**12.** 24 and 36
13. 26 and 39	**14.** 33 and 22	**15.** 15 and 30
16. 14 and 28		

Name: _____ Date: _____

NCTM Standard: Number and Operations – understand ways of representing numbers and work flexibly with fractions

Clip Lowest Common Denominators

30 ___	4 ___	45 ___	40 ___
18 ___	9 ___	6 ___	72 ___
56 ___	12 ___	24 ___	35 ___
28 ___	20 ___	15 ___	21 ___

Find the least common denominator for each pair of fractions below, and then find the answer in the boxes above. Write the item number on the line in the box that has the correct answer.

1. $\frac{1}{2}$ and $\frac{1}{4}$ **2.** $\frac{3}{8}$ and $\frac{4}{9}$ **3.** $\frac{1}{4}$ and $\frac{5}{6}$ **4.** $\frac{5}{9}$ and $\frac{5}{6}$

5. $\frac{6}{7}$ and $\frac{2}{3}$ **6.** $\frac{3}{8}$ and $\frac{4}{5}$ **7.** $\frac{3}{4}$ and $\frac{3}{7}$ **8.** $\frac{5}{6}$ and $\frac{3}{8}$

9. $\frac{2}{3}$ and $\frac{2}{9}$ **10.** $\frac{3}{5}$ and $\frac{1}{4}$ **11.** $\frac{1}{5}$ and $\frac{2}{3}$ **12.** $\frac{1}{6}$ and $\frac{1}{3}$

13. $\frac{5}{9}$ and $\frac{2}{5}$ **14.** $\frac{7}{8}$ and $\frac{6}{7}$ **15.** $\frac{1}{5}$ and $\frac{2}{7}$ **16.** $\frac{2}{5}$ and $\frac{5}{6}$

Name: _____ Date: _____

NCTM Standard: Number and Operations – understand ways of representing numbers and work flexibly with fractions

Conquest Over Common Denominators

____ $\frac{1}{4}$ and $\frac{1}{2}$	____ $\frac{1}{4}$ and $\frac{2}{3}$	____ $\frac{2}{5}$ and $\frac{1}{2}$	____ $\frac{3}{4}$ and $\frac{4}{5}$
____ $\frac{2}{3}$ and $\frac{5}{6}$	____ $\frac{1}{5}$ and $\frac{1}{4}$	____ $\frac{1}{5}$ and $\frac{1}{3}$	____ $\frac{1}{2}$ and $\frac{4}{5}$
____ $\frac{1}{3}$ and $\frac{5}{6}$	____ $\frac{3}{4}$ and $\frac{1}{3}$	____ $\frac{1}{4}$ and $\frac{1}{3}$	____ $\frac{2}{5}$ and $\frac{2}{3}$
____ $\frac{3}{4}$ and $\frac{2}{5}$	____ $\frac{1}{6}$ and $\frac{1}{3}$	____ $\frac{4}{5}$ and $\frac{1}{3}$	____ $\frac{4}{5}$ and $\frac{1}{4}$

Reduce each pair of fractions to lowest terms, and then find the matching pair in the boxes above. Write the item number on the line in the box that has the correct answer.

1. $\frac{4}{20}$ and $\frac{5}{20}$
2. $\frac{4}{10}$ and $\frac{5}{10}$
3. $\frac{1}{4}$ and $\frac{2}{4}$
4. $\frac{15}{20}$ and $\frac{16}{20}$
5. $\frac{15}{20}$ and $\frac{8}{20}$
6. $\frac{5}{10}$ and $\frac{8}{10}$
7. $\frac{9}{12}$ and $\frac{4}{12}$
8. $\frac{3}{12}$ and $\frac{4}{12}$
9. $\frac{3}{12}$ and $\frac{8}{12}$
10. $\frac{1}{6}$ and $\frac{2}{6}$
11. $\frac{2}{6}$ and $\frac{5}{6}$
12. $\frac{4}{6}$ and $\frac{5}{6}$
13. $\frac{12}{15}$ and $\frac{5}{15}$
14. $\frac{6}{15}$ and $\frac{10}{15}$
15. $\frac{16}{20}$ and $\frac{5}{20}$
16. $\frac{3}{15}$ and $\frac{5}{15}$

Name: _____ Date: _____

NCTM Standard: Number and Operations – compute fluently and work flexibly with fractions

Find an Improper Fraction

$\dfrac{15}{7}$ ___	$\dfrac{53}{4}$ ___	$\dfrac{23}{7}$ ___	$\dfrac{23}{3}$ ___
$\dfrac{12}{7}$ ___	$\dfrac{16}{5}$ ___	$\dfrac{13}{8}$ ___	$\dfrac{25}{6}$ ___
$\dfrac{14}{8}$ ___	$\dfrac{17}{9}$ ___	$\dfrac{11}{3}$ ___	$\dfrac{68}{9}$ ___
$\dfrac{77}{5}$ ___	$\dfrac{34}{9}$ ___	$\dfrac{44}{9}$ ___	$\dfrac{62}{7}$ ___

Match each mixed number below with an improper fraction in the boxes above. Write the item number on the line in the box that has the correct answer.

1. $3\frac{2}{3}$ **2.** $3\frac{7}{9}$ **3.** $1\frac{5}{7}$ **4.** $7\frac{2}{3}$

5. $2\frac{1}{7}$ **6.** $1\frac{8}{9}$ **7.** $4\frac{1}{6}$ **8.** $3\frac{1}{5}$

9. $15\frac{2}{5}$ **10.** $8\frac{6}{7}$ **11.** $13\frac{1}{4}$ **12.** $1\frac{6}{8}$

13. $1\frac{5}{8}$ **14.** $4\frac{8}{9}$ **15.** $3\frac{2}{7}$ **16.** $7\frac{5}{9}$

Name: _____   Date: _____

NCTM Standard: Number and Operations – understand fractions as part of a collection

Hook Fractions as Part of a Collection

$\frac{4}{11}$ ___	$\frac{7}{10}$ ___	$\frac{2}{3}$ ___	$\frac{8}{9}$ ___
$\frac{4}{7}$ ___	$\frac{1}{2}$ ___	$\frac{3}{10}$ ___	$\frac{7}{11}$ ___
$\frac{5}{12}$ ___	$\frac{5}{9}$ ___	$\frac{6}{11}$ ___	$\frac{8}{11}$ ___
$\frac{4}{5}$ ___	$\frac{3}{4}$ ___	$\frac{3}{8}$ ___	$\frac{7}{12}$ ___

Name each fraction that is represented by the gray shapes below, and then find the answer in lowest terms in the boxes above. Write the item number on the line in the box that has the correct answer.

1. ▨▨▨▨▨▨□□□□□□

2. □□□□▨▨▨▨▨

3. ▨▨▨▨▨▨▨□□□

4. ▨▨▨▨□□□□□□

5. □□□▨▨▨▨▨▨

6. □▨▨□□□□□▨

7. ▨▨▨▨▨□□□□

8. □□□▨▨▨▨▨▨▨

9. ▨▨▨▨▨▨▨□

10. ▨▨▨□□□□□▨▨▨

11. ▨▨▨□□□□

12. □□▨▨▨▨▨

13. ▨▨▨□□□

14. □□□▨▨▨

15. ▨▨▨▨▨▨▨▨□□

16. ▨▨▨□□□□▨▨▨

Name: _____ Date: _____

NCTM Standard: Number and Operations – understand fractions as part of a collection

Lasso Fractions in a Collection

$\frac{3}{7}$ ___	$\frac{5}{13}$ ___	$\frac{6}{17}$ ___	$\frac{4}{11}$ ___
$\frac{2}{3}$ ___	$\frac{9}{14}$ ___	$\frac{6}{13}$ ___	$\frac{1}{3}$ ___
$\frac{6}{7}$ ___	$\frac{1}{2}$ ___	$\frac{1}{6}$ ___	$\frac{2}{5}$ ___
$\frac{4}{5}$ ___	$\frac{1}{5}$ ___	$\frac{3}{5}$ ___	$\frac{1}{4}$ ___

Name each fraction that is represented by the black dots below, reduce the fraction to lowest terms, and then find the answer in the boxes above. Write the item number on the line in the box that has the correct answer.

1.

2.

3.

4.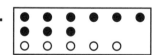

5.

6.

7.

8.

9.

10.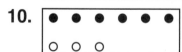

11.

12.

13.

14.

15.

16.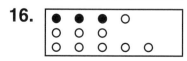

Name: _____ Date: _____

NCTM Standard: Number and Operations – understand ways of
representing numbers and work flexibly with fractions

Reduce Those Fractions!

**Using the black dots as the numerator and the gray dots as the denominator,
reduce the fraction to lowest terms, and then find the answer in the boxes
at the right. Write the item number on the line in the box that has the correct
answer.**

1. ● ● ● ● ● ● ● ● ● ● ● ● ● ● ● ●
   ○ ○ ○ ○ ○ ○ ○ ○ ○ ○ ○ ○ ○ ○

2. ● ● ● ● ● ● ● ● ● ● ● ● ●
   ○ ○ ○ ○ ○ ○ ○ ○ ○ ○ ○ ○ ○ ○ ○ ○

3. ● ● ● ● ● ●
   ○ ○ ○ ○ ○ ○ ○ ○ ○ ○ ○ ○ ○ ○ ○

4. ● ● ● ● ● ● ● ● ● ● ● ● ● ● ●
   ○ ○ ○ ○ ○ ○ ○ ○ ○ ○ ○ ○ ○ ○ ○ ○ ○ ○

5. ● ● ● ● ●
   ○ ○ ○ ○ ○ ○ ○ ○ ○ ○ ○ ○ ○ ○ ○

6. ● ● ● ● ● ● ● ● ● ● ● ●
   ○ ○ ○ ○ ○ ○ ○ ○ ○

7. ● ● ● ● ● ● ● ● ● ● ● ● ● ● ● ●
   ○ ○ ○ ○ ○ ○ ○ ○ ○ ○ ○ ○ ○

8. ● ● ● ● ● ● ● ● ● ● ● ● ● ● ● ●
   ○ ○ ○ ○ ○ ○ ○ ○ ○ ○ ○ ○ ○ ○

9. ● ● ● ● ● ● ● ● ● ● ● ● ● ●
   ○ ○ ○ ○ ○ ○ ○ ○ ○ ○ ○

10. ● ● ● ● ● ● ● ● ● ● ● ● ●
    ○ ○ ○ ○ ○ ○ ○ ○ ○ ○ ○ ○ ○ ○ ○

11. ● ● ●
    ○ ○ ○ ○ ○ ○ ○ ○ ○ ○ ○ ○ ○ ○ ○ ○

12. ● ● ● ● ● ● ● ● ●
    ○ ○ ○ ○ ○ ○ ○ ○ ○ ○ ○

13. ● ● ● ● ● ● ● ●
    ○ ○ ○ ○ ○ ○ ○ ○ ○ ○ ○ ○ ○ ○ ○ ○

14. ● ● ● ● ● ● ● ● ● ●
    ○ ○ ○ ○ ○ ○ ○ ○ ○ ○ ○ ○ ○ ○ ○ ○ ○ ○

15. ● ● ● ●
    ○ ○ ○ ○ ○ ○ ○ ○ ○ ○ ○ ○

16. ● ● ● ● ● ● ●
    ○ ○ ○ ○ ○ ○ ○ ○ ○ ○ ○ ○

$\frac{1}{5}$ ___	$\frac{4}{7}$ ___
$\frac{8}{9}$ ___	$1\frac{1}{8}$ ___
$\frac{3}{5}$ ___	$1\frac{1}{4}$ ___
$1\frac{2}{3}$ ___	$1\frac{1}{2}$ ___
$\frac{2}{5}$ ___	$\frac{1}{4}$ ___
$\frac{1}{3}$ ___	$\frac{4}{9}$ ___
$1\frac{1}{5}$ ___	$\frac{5}{6}$ ___
$\frac{4}{5}$ ___	$\frac{7}{9}$ ___

Name: _____ Date: _____

NCTM Standard: Number and Operations – understand ways of representing numbers

Snatch the Least Common Multiple

36 ___	12 ___	42 ___
60 ___	40 ___	30 ___
16 ___	10 ___	8 ___
72 ___	90 ___	28 ___
15 ___	6 ___	18 ___

Find the least common multiple of each of the following pairs of numbers in the boxes above. Write the item number on the line in the box that has the correct answer.

1. 8 and 4   **2.** 9 and 4   **3.** 8 and 5

4. 9 and 10   **5.** 6 and 4   **6.** 6 and 3

7. 8 and 16   **8.** 8 and 9   **9.** 9 and 6

10. 4 and 7   **11.** 5 and 10   **12.** 5 and 3

13. 15 and 10   **14.** 14 and 21   **15.** 12 and 20

UNIT 6

Name: _____   Date: _____

NCTM Standard: Number and Operations – understand fractions as part of a collection and on a number line

Secure Some Fractions

$2\frac{3}{8}$ ___	$3\frac{1}{4}$ ___	6 ___	$3\frac{3}{8}$ ___
$2\frac{2}{16}$ ___	$7\frac{3}{4}$ ___	$2\frac{1}{8}$ ___	5 ___
$1\frac{1}{4}$ ___	$5\frac{7}{8}$ ___	$1\frac{5}{8}$ ___	$4\frac{3}{4}$ ___
$5\frac{2}{8}$ ___	$4\frac{5}{8}$ ___	$2\frac{3}{4}$ ___	$1\frac{2}{8}$ ___

Determine the fraction that would be at the arrow on each number line below, and then find that fraction in the boxes above. Write the item number on the line in the box that has the correct answer.

1. 5 ———↑——— 7 **2.** 7 ———————↑— 8

3. 1 ———↑——— $1\frac{1}{2}$ **4.** $2\frac{1}{2}$ ————↑——— 3

5. 4 ————↑——— 6 **6.** $1\frac{1}{2}$ ————↑——— $1\frac{3}{4}$

7. $2\frac{1}{4}$ ————↑——— $2\frac{1}{2}$ **8.** $1\frac{1}{8}$ ————↑——— $1\frac{3}{8}$

9. $2\frac{1}{16}$ ————↑——— $2\frac{3}{16}$ **10.** $3\frac{1}{4}$ ————↑——— $3\frac{4}{8}$

11. $4\frac{1}{2}$ —↑——————— 5 **12.** 2 ————↑——— $2\frac{1}{4}$

13. 3 ————↑——— $3\frac{1}{2}$ **14.** 4 —————↑—— 5

15. $5\frac{1}{2}$ —————↑—— 6 **16.** $5\frac{1}{8}$ —————↑—— $5\frac{3}{8}$

UNIT 6

Name: _____ Date: _____

NCTM Standard: Number and Operations – understand ways of representing numbers

Grasp a Fractional Location

$4\frac{1}{4}$ ___	$1\frac{1}{16}$ ___	$2\frac{1}{8}$ ___	$2\frac{3}{4}$ ___
$6\frac{3}{4}$ ___	$1\frac{1}{4}$ ___	4 ___	$7\frac{1}{2}$ ___
$3\frac{1}{2}$ ___	$10\frac{1}{8}$ ___	$\frac{3}{4}$ ___	$7\frac{3}{4}$ ___
$\frac{2}{4}$ ___	8 ___	$4\frac{1}{3}$ ___	6 ___

The lines below represent some fractions. In the boxes above, find the fraction that would be where the arrow is located. Write the item number on the line in the box that has the correct answer.

1. $\frac{1}{4}$ —————↑————— $\frac{3}{4}$ **2.** $\frac{1}{2}$ —————↑————— 1

3. 1 ———↑——————— 2 **4.** 2 —————————↑— 3

5. 4 —————↑——— $4\frac{1}{2}$ **6.** 5 —————↑——— 7

7. 10 —↑————————— 11 **8.** 3 ————↑——————— 6

9. 6 ————↑——————— 9 **10.** 7 ———↑————————— 11

11. 1 ——↑——————— $1\frac{1}{2}$ **12.** 2 —————↑——— $2\frac{1}{4}$

13. 3 ————↑————— 4 **14.** 4 ———↑————————— 5

15. 6 ———————↑—— 7 **16.** 7 ——————————↑— 8

Name: _____ Date: _____

NCTM Standard: Number and Operations – understand ways of representing numbers and work flexibly with fractions

---

Stamp Out Common Denominators

____ $\frac{3}{15}$ and $\frac{10}{15}$	____ $\frac{20}{24}$ and $\frac{9}{24}$	____ $\frac{1}{6}$ and $\frac{2}{6}$
____ $\frac{3}{12}$ and $\frac{10}{12}$	____ $\frac{49}{56}$ and $\frac{48}{56}$	____ $\frac{10}{18}$ and $\frac{15}{18}$
____ $\frac{6}{9}$ and $\frac{2}{9}$	____ $\frac{18}{21}$ and $\frac{14}{21}$	____ $\frac{3}{9}$ and $\frac{2}{9}$
____ $\frac{15}{40}$ and $\frac{32}{40}$	____ $\frac{21}{28}$ and $\frac{12}{28}$	____ $\frac{27}{72}$ and $\frac{16}{72}$
____ $\frac{2}{4}$ and $\frac{1}{4}$	____ $\frac{25}{45}$ and $\frac{18}{45}$	____ $\frac{12}{20}$ and $\frac{5}{20}$

UNIT 6

For each pair of fractions below, find the fractions with the common denominators in the boxes above. Write the item number on the line in the box that has the correct answer.

1. $\frac{6}{7}$ and $\frac{2}{3}$ 2. $\frac{1}{4}$ and $\frac{5}{6}$ 3. $\frac{1}{2}$ and $\frac{1}{4}$

4. $\frac{2}{3}$ and $\frac{2}{9}$ 5. $\frac{3}{4}$ and $\frac{3}{7}$ 6. $\frac{1}{6}$ and $\frac{1}{3}$

7. $\frac{7}{8}$ and $\frac{6}{7}$ 8. $\frac{1}{5}$ and $\frac{2}{3}$ 9. $\frac{3}{5}$ and $\frac{1}{4}$

10. $\frac{1}{3}$ and $\frac{2}{9}$ 11. $\frac{5}{9}$ and $\frac{2}{5}$ 12. $\frac{5}{6}$ and $\frac{3}{8}$

13. $\frac{3}{8}$ and $\frac{4}{5}$ 14. $\frac{5}{9}$ and $\frac{5}{6}$ 15. $\frac{3}{8}$ and $\frac{2}{9}$

Name: _____ Date: _____

NCTM Standard: Number and Operations – compute fluently

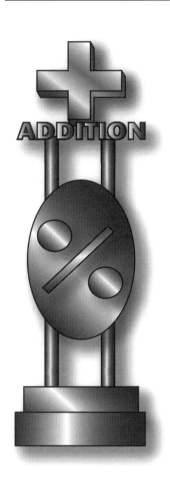

Triumph Over Adding Fractions

$\frac{7}{10}$ ___	$\frac{4}{9}$ ___	$1\frac{3}{10}$ ___	$\frac{3}{4}$ ___
$1\frac{2}{5}$ ___	1 ___	$1\frac{1}{3}$ ___	$1\frac{1}{5}$ ___
$\frac{2}{3}$ ___	$\frac{1}{2}$ ___	$\frac{7}{8}$ ___	$1\frac{3}{5}$ ___
$\frac{11}{15}$ ___	$1\frac{1}{7}$ ___	$1\frac{1}{6}$ ___	$1\frac{1}{2}$ ___

Solve each problem below, reduce to lowest terms, and then find the answer in the boxes above. Write the item number on the line in the box that has the correct answer.

1. $\frac{1}{2} + \frac{1}{2} =$ 2. $\frac{1}{4} + \frac{2}{4} =$ 3. $\frac{4}{5} + \frac{3}{5} =$

4. $\frac{2}{8} + \frac{5}{8} =$ 5. $\frac{1}{3} + \frac{1}{3} =$ 6. $\frac{3}{10} + \frac{4}{10} =$

7. $\frac{1}{6} + \frac{2}{6} =$ 8. $\frac{7}{10} + \frac{9}{10} =$ 9. $\frac{3}{4} + \frac{3}{4} =$

10. $\frac{6}{10} + \frac{7}{10} =$ 11. $\frac{5}{6} + \frac{3}{6} =$ 12. $\frac{5}{7} + \frac{3}{7} =$

13. $\frac{5}{12} + \frac{9}{12} =$ 14. $\frac{4}{15} + \frac{7}{15} =$ 15. $\frac{6}{15} + \frac{12}{15} =$

16. $\frac{5}{18} + \frac{3}{18} =$

Name: _____   Date: _____

NCTM Standard: Number and Operations – compute fluently and make reasonable estimates; use mental computation to estimate fractions

Bring in a Flood of Quotients

11 __	18 __	6 __	49 __
42 __	23 __	9 __	55 __
2 __	10 __	14 __	52 __
5 __	26 __	7 __	3 __

See if you can solve the following fraction problems by "visualizing" the dividend. Then find the answer in the boxes above. Write the item number on the line in the box that has the correct answer.

1. $2\frac{1}{2} \div \frac{1}{2} =$ 2. $2\frac{1}{2} \div \frac{1}{4} =$ 3. $6\frac{1}{8} \div \frac{1}{8} =$

4. $2\frac{3}{4} \div \frac{1}{4} =$ 5. $2\frac{1}{4} \div \frac{3}{4} =$ 6. $3\frac{1}{2} \div \frac{1}{4} =$

7. $6\frac{7}{8} \div \frac{1}{8} =$ 8. $4\frac{1}{2} \div \frac{1}{2} =$ 9. $6\frac{1}{2} \div \frac{1}{4} =$

10. $3\frac{1}{2} \div \frac{1}{2} =$ 11. $4\frac{1}{2} \div \frac{1}{4} =$ 12. $1\frac{1}{2} \div \frac{1}{4} =$

13. $5\frac{1}{4} \div \frac{1}{8} =$ 14. $6\frac{1}{2} \div \frac{1}{8} =$ 15. $1\frac{1}{2} \div \frac{3}{4} =$

16. $2\frac{7}{8} \div \frac{1}{8} =$

Name: _____   Date: _____

NCTM Standard: Number and Operations – compute fluently and use mental calculation to compute fractions

Win a Product

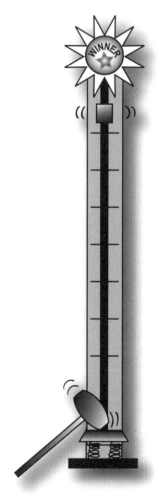

120 ___	**10** ___	**45** ___
20 ___	**12** ___	**5** ___
4 ___	**35** ___	**18** ___
6 ___	**25** ___	**30** ___
150 ___	**75** ___	**60** ___

Multiply the fractions and whole numbers in the problems below. Then find the answers in the boxes above. Write the item number on the line in the box that has the correct answer.

1. $\frac{1}{2}$ x 70   =   **2.** $\frac{1}{2}$ x 90   =   **3.** $\frac{3}{4}$ x 80   =

4. $\frac{3}{4}$ x 200 =   **5.** $\frac{1}{2}$ x 50   =   **6.** $\frac{1}{2}$ x 24   =

7. $\frac{3}{4}$ x 24   =   **8.** $\frac{3}{4}$ x 160 =   **9.** $\frac{1}{2}$ x 150 =

10. $\frac{1}{5}$ x 150 =   **11.** $\frac{1}{5}$ x 20   =   **12.** $\frac{1}{5}$ x 30   =

13. $\frac{1}{4}$ x 20   =   **14.** $\frac{1}{4}$ x 80   =   **15.** $\frac{1}{5}$ x 50   =

Name: _____ Date: _____

NCTM Standard: Number and Operations – compute fluently and make reasonable estimates; use mental computation to estimate fractions

Conquer Multiplying Mixed Numbers

$11\frac{1}{4}$ ___	10 ___	9 ___	18 ___
$10\frac{1}{2}$ ___	22 ___	3 ___	8 ___
$4\frac{1}{2}$ ___	15 ___	$3\frac{1}{2}$ ___	17 ___
$13\frac{1}{2}$ ___	12 ___	$7\frac{1}{2}$ ___	14 ___

Multiply the mixed numbers times the whole numbers below, and find the answers in the boxes above. Write the item number on the line in the box that has the correct answer.

1. $2\frac{1}{2}$ x 6 =

2. $1\frac{1}{2}$ x 2 =

3. $3\frac{1}{2}$ x 3 =

4. $2\frac{1}{4}$ x 4 =

5. $2\frac{1}{4}$ x 8 =

6. $1\frac{1}{2}$ x 3 =

7. $1\frac{1}{2}$ x 5 =

8. $2\frac{1}{8}$ x 8 =

9. $1\frac{1}{4}$ x 9 =

10. $3\frac{1}{3}$ x 3 =

11. $1\frac{1}{2}$ x 9 =

12. $2\frac{1}{3}$ x 6 =

13. $1\frac{1}{3}$ x 6 =

14. $1\frac{1}{5}$ x 10 =

15. $2\frac{1}{5}$ x 10 =

16. $3\frac{1}{2}$ x 1 =

Name: _____ Date: _____

NCTM Standard: Number and Operations – compute fluently; select appropriate methods for fraction computation

Finding Fractional Parts of Whole Numbers

100 __	24 __	60 __	20 __
5 __	6 __	45 __	10 __
30 __	27 __	4 __	11 __
40 __	50 __	70 __	12 __

Find the fractional part of each whole number in the problems below, and find the answer in the boxes above. Write the item number on the line in the box that has the correct answer.

1. $\frac{1}{2}$ of 12 =   **2.** $\frac{1}{4}$ of 16 =   **3.** $\frac{1}{5}$ of 25 =

4. $\frac{1}{2}$ of 60 =   **5.** $\frac{1}{5}$ of 50 =   **6.** $\frac{1}{3}$ of 36 =

7. $\frac{1}{2}$ of 48 =   **8.** $\frac{1}{3}$ of 150 =   **9.** $\frac{1}{4}$ of 44 =

10. $\frac{1}{4}$ of 400 =   **11.** $\frac{1}{5}$ of 100 =   **12.** $\frac{1}{2}$ of 90 =

13. $\frac{1}{4}$ of 160 =   **14.** $\frac{1}{5}$ of 350 =

15. $\frac{1}{3}$ of 81 =   **16.** $\frac{1}{3}$ of 180 =

Name: _____   Date: _____

NCTM Standard: Number and Operations – understand ways of representing numbers and work flexibly with fractions, decimals, and percents

Button Down Fractions and Decimals

6.2 ___	**0.2** ___	**3.5** ___
5.25 ___	**1.2** ___	**3.25** ___
1.25 ___	**1.5** ___	**1.125** ___
3.625 ___	**5.2** ___	**0.5** ___
3.375 ___	**3.125** ___	**1.4** ___

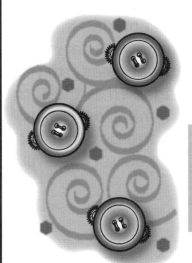

For each of the fractions below, find the corresponding decimal in the boxes above. Write the item number on the line in the box that has the correct answer.

1. $1\frac{1}{2}$ 2. $3\frac{1}{4}$ 3. $3\frac{1}{8}$ 4. $5\frac{2}{8}$ 5. $1\frac{1}{4}$

6. $\frac{1}{2}$ 7. $\frac{1}{5}$ 8. $1\frac{1}{5}$ 9. $3\frac{1}{2}$ 10. $5\frac{1}{5}$

11. $6\frac{1}{5}$ 12. $1\frac{1}{8}$ 13. $3\frac{3}{8}$ 14. $1\frac{2}{5}$ 15. $3\frac{5}{8}$

Math Games: Grades 5–6 — Unit 7: Fraction, Decimal, and Percent Equivalents

Name: _____ Date: _____

NCTM Standard: Number and Operations – compute fluently and make reasonable estimates

UNIT 7

Strike Out Some Mixed Numbers

For each decimal below, find the corresponding fraction in lowest terms in the boxes to the right. Write the item number on the line in the box that has the correct answer.

$5\frac{3}{8}$ ___	$5\frac{1}{20}$ ___	$2\frac{3}{5}$ ___	$3\frac{3}{4}$ ___	$2\frac{1}{4}$ ___
$7\frac{4}{5}$ ___	$5\frac{1}{4}$ ___	$5\frac{3}{4}$ ___	$7\frac{1}{20}$ ___	$5\frac{1}{10}$ ___
$5\frac{1}{2}$ ___	$7\frac{1}{4}$ ___	$3\frac{1}{2}$ ___	$7\frac{1}{5}$ ___	$7\frac{1}{2}$ ___
$3\frac{3}{8}$ ___	$2\frac{1}{2}$ ___	$1\frac{11}{20}$ ___	$2\frac{3}{4}$ ___	$5\frac{1}{8}$ ___
$3\frac{9}{10}$ ___	$3\frac{1}{4}$ ___	$5\frac{1}{5}$ ___	$7\frac{1}{8}$ ___	$5\frac{5}{8}$ ___

1. 5.25
2. 3.5
3. 1.55
4. 3.75
5. 5.5
6. 3.25
7. 5.125
8. 5.375
9. 7.05
10. 5.05
11. 7.125
12. 3.375
13. 2.25
14. 7.5
15. 5.625
16. 2.75
17. 5.75
18. 7.25
19. 2.5
20. 5.1
21. 7.2
22. 5.2
23. 2.6
24. 7.8
25. 3.9

Name: _____ Date: _____

NCTM Standard: Number and Operations – understand ways of representing numbers; work flexibly with fractions and decimals

---

Finding Fraction-Decimal Equivalents

$\frac{2}{10}$ ____	$\frac{40}{1000}$ ____	$\frac{20}{1000}$ ____
$\frac{5}{100}$ ____	$\frac{6}{10}$ ____	$\frac{5}{10}$ ____
$\frac{4}{10}$ ____	$\frac{8}{10}$ ____	$\frac{8}{1000}$ ____
$\frac{6}{100}$ ____	$\frac{25}{100}$ ____	$\frac{6}{1000}$ ____
$\frac{25}{1000}$ ____	$\frac{2}{100}$ ____	$\frac{8}{100}$ ____

Find the fraction equivalents of the following decimals in the boxes above. Write the item number on the line in the box that has the correct answer.

1. 0.25	**2.** 0.5	**3.** 0.4	**4.** 0.2
5. 0.02	**6.** 0.05	**7.** 0.8	**8.** 0.025
9. 0.040	**10.** 0.08	**11.** 0.6	**12.** 0.020
13. 0.06	**14.** 0.008	**15.** 0.006	

Name: _____ Date: _____

NCTM Standard: Number and Operations – understand ways of representing numbers; work flexibly with fractions, decimals, and percents

Grab on to Fraction-Decimal-Percent Equivalents

UNIT 7

$\frac{7}{8}$	40%	0.8	$\frac{9}{20}$
20%	$\frac{3}{5}$	25%	$\frac{1}{2}$
$\frac{7}{20}$	$\frac{1}{8}$	$\frac{2}{5}$	$\frac{7}{10}$
0.75	62.5%	90%	0.6

In each item below are two equivalent fractions, decimals, or percents. Find the third matching equivalent for each item in the boxes above. Write the item number on the line in the box that has the correct answer.

1. 50%   0.50   _____
2. $\frac{3}{4}$ 75%   _____
3. 45%   0.45   _____
4. 0.2 $\frac{1}{5}$ _____
5. 80% $\frac{4}{5}$ _____
6. 0.40   40%   _____
7. 60% $\frac{3}{5}$ _____
8. $\frac{2}{5}$ 0.4   _____
9. $\frac{5}{8}$ 0.625   _____
10. 87.5%   0.875   _____
11. 60%   0.6   _____
12. 0.35   35%   _____
13. $\frac{1}{4}$ 0.25   _____
14. 12.5%   0.125   _____
15. 70%   0.7   _____
16. 0.9 $\frac{9}{10}$ _____

Name: _____ Date: _____

NCTM Standard: Number and Operations – understand ways of representing numbers and work flexibly with fractions, decimals, and percents

Collar Some Multiples

4 ___	30 ___	16 ___	15 ___
60 ___	2 ___	10 ___	5 ___
75 ___	70 ___	50 ___	2.5 ___
100 ___	45 ___	20 ___	25 ___

Mentally calculate each problem below, and then find the answer in the boxes above. Write the item number on the line in the box that has the correct answer.

1. 25% of 400 =

2. $\frac{1}{2}$ of 40 =

3. 0.1 of 20 =

4. 50% of 30 =

5. 75% of 80 =

6. $\frac{1}{3}$ of 90 =

7. 0.5 of 50 =

8. 50% of 150 =

9. 25% of 20 =

10. $\frac{1}{4}$ of 200 =

11. $\frac{1}{5}$ of 50 =

12. $\frac{1}{3}$ of 210 =

13. 0.4 of 10 =

14. 0.25 of 10 =

15. 0.5 of 90 =

16. 20% of 80 =

Name: _____ Date: _____

NCTM Standard: Number and Operations – understand ways of representing numbers and work flexibly with fractions, decimals, and percents

UNIT 7

Salvage Lots of Percent Equivalents

_____ 225%	_____ 75%	_____ 37.5%	_____ 275%
_____ 12.5%	_____ 30%	_____ 20%	_____ 25%
_____ 60%	_____ 50%	_____ 87.5%	_____ 150%
_____ 40%	_____ 125%	_____ 80%	_____ 62.5%

For each fraction below, find the corresponding percentage in the boxes above. Write the item number on the line in the box that has the correct answer.

1. $\frac{1}{2}$

2. $\frac{1}{4}$

3. $\frac{1}{5}$

4. $\frac{2}{5}$

5. $\frac{4}{5}$

6. $\frac{3}{4}$

7. $\frac{1}{8}$

8. $1\frac{1}{2}$

9. $2\frac{1}{4}$

10. $1\frac{1}{4}$

11. $2\frac{3}{4}$

12. $\frac{3}{5}$

13. $\frac{3}{8}$

14. $\frac{5}{8}$

15. $\frac{7}{8}$

16. $\frac{3}{10}$

Name: _____   Date: _____

NCTM Standard: Number and Operations – compute fluently; work flexibly with percents to solve problems or estimate answers

Pounce on a Percent

1 ___	**20** ___	**15** ___	**40** ___
3 ___	**4** ___	**2** ___	**14** ___
21 ___	**10** ___	**5** ___	**9** ___
12 ___	**30** ___	**8** ___	**50** ___

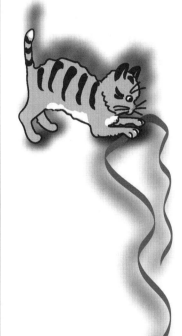

Find the answer to each problem below in the boxes above. Write the item number on the line in the box that has the correct answer.

1. 2% of 100 =   2. 25% of 12 =
3. 50% of 20 =   4. 50% of 80 =
5. 50% of 100 =   6. 25% of 120 =
7. 25% of 4 =   8. 25% of 36 =
9. 75% of 28 =   10. 75% of 16 =
11. 75% of 20 =   12. 20% of 100 =
13. 20% of 40 =   14. 20% of 70 =
15. 25% of 20 =   16. 5% of 80 =

Name: _____   Date: _____

NCTM Standard: Number and Operations – understand ways of representing numbers and work flexibly with percents

Round Up Percents

Find what percent the black dots are in relation to the gray dots for each of the problems below, and then find the answer in the boxes to the right. Write the item number on the line in the box that has the correct answer.

1.
2.
3.
4.
5.
6.
7.
8.
9.
10.
11.
12.
13.
14.
15.

___ 90%	___ 100%	___ 120%
___ 50%	___ 10%	___ 70%
___ 140%	___ 20%	___ 80%
___ 130%	___ 150%	___ 110%
___ 30%	___ 60%	___ 40%

UNIT 8

Name: _____ Date: _____

NCTM Standard: Number and Operations – understand ways of representing numbers and work flexibly with fractions, decimals, and percents

Snare Sale Prices

——	——	——	——
$16	$20	$105	$22.50
——	——	——	——
$140	$375	$1,600	$6.25
——	——	——	——
$875	$10	$17.50	$15
——	——	——	——
$90	$175	$28	$50

You are all familiar with store sales. Below are some items that have been reduced in a store. Find out how much money would be taken off of each item, and then find the answers in the boxes above. Write the item number on the line in the box that has the correct answer.

1. 30% off of $300.00
2. 25% off of $70.00
3. 40% off of $50.00
4. 35% off of $2,500.00
5. 25% off of $25.00
6. 20% off of $80.00
7. 25% off of $200.00
8. 75% off of $500.00
9. 75% off of $30.00
10. 25% off of $700.00
11. 20% off of $700.00
12. 25% off of $60.00
13. 25% off of $40.00
14. 35% off of $300.00
15. 40% off of $70.00
16. 20% off of $8,000.00

Name: _____ Date: _____

NCTM Standard: Number and Operations – compute fluently; work flexibly with percents to solve problems; make reasonable estimates

Tag the Percent One Number Is of Another Number

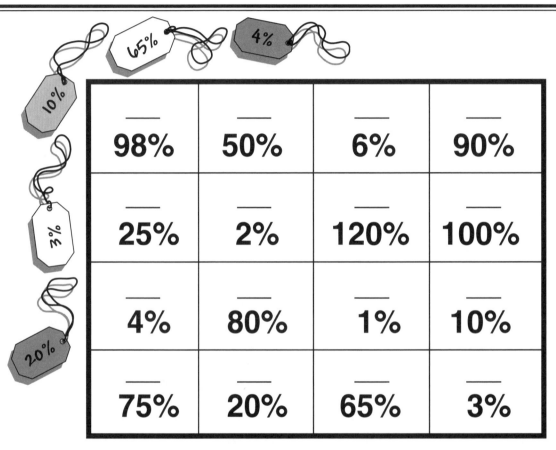

Solve the problems below, and find the answers in the boxes above. Write the item number on the line in the box that has the correct answer.

1. What percent is 1 of 100?
2. What percent is 2 of 100?
3. What percent is 8 of 200?
4. What percent is 10 of 50?
5. What percent is 2 of 2?
6. What percent is 20 of 40?
7. What percent is 65 of 100?
8. What percent is 10 of 40?
9. What percent is 98 of 100?
10. What percent is 2 of 20?
11. What percent is 30 of 500?
12. What percent is 3 of 100?
13. What percent is 12 of 10?
14. What percent is 4 of 5?
15. What percent is 6 of 8?
16. What percent is 9 of 10?

Name: _____ Date: _____

NCTM Standard: Number and Operations – understand ways of representing numbers and work flexibly with fractions, decimals, and percents

Wrap Up a Raise

Below is a chart showing hourly, daily, weekly, or monthly wage. In the second column, it shows the percent increase in the salary the person will receive. Find the resulting wage <u>after</u> the increase in the boxes at the right. Write the item number on the line in the box that has the correct answer.

Wage	Percent Increase
1. $5.00 per hour	2%
2. $200.00 per week	3%
3. $200.00 per month	10%
4. $500.00 per month	8%
5. $7.00 per hour	3%
6. $40.00 per day	6%
7. $300.00 per week	10%
8. $300.00 per month	5%
9. $200.00 per month	15%
10. $10.00 per hour	2%
11. $400.00 per week	5%
12. $400.00 per month	12%
13. $500.00 per week	6%
14. $20.00 per hour	8%
15. $400.00 per month	15%
16. $600.00 per month	10%

$530 ___	$10.20 ___
$42.40 ___	$660 ___
$540 ___	$460 ___
$220 ___	$21.60 ___
$315 ___	$5.10 ___
$330 ___	$420 ___
$230 ___	$206 ___
$7.21 ___	$448 ___

Name: _____ Date: _____

NCTM Standard: Number and Operations – understand and use ratios to represent quantitative relationships

Draw in Ratios

Determine the ratio of black dots to gray dots for each of the problems below, and then find the answer in lowest terms in the boxes to the right. Write the item number on the line in the box that has the correct answer.

1.
2.
3.
4.
5.
6.
7.
8.
9.
10.
11.
12.
13.
14.
15.

$\dfrac{7}{9}$	$5\dfrac{2}{3}$	$1\dfrac{3}{11}$
$\dfrac{5}{9}$	$\dfrac{1}{4}$	$1\dfrac{4}{11}$
$2\dfrac{1}{8}$	1	$\dfrac{3}{4}$
$1\dfrac{1}{4}$	$\dfrac{12}{17}$	$1\dfrac{4}{9}$
$\dfrac{10}{11}$	2	$3\dfrac{2}{5}$

Name: _____ Date: _____

NCTM Standard: Number and Operations – understand ways of representing numbers and work flexibly with ratios

Rack Up Ratios

Determine the ratio of black dots to gray dots, and then find the ratio in lowest terms in the boxes to the right. Write the item number on the line in the box that has the correct answer.

1.
2.
3.
4.
5.
6.
7.
8.
9.
10.
11.
12.
13.
14.
15.

___	___	___
3:1	**5:2**	**5:12**
___	___	___
13:8	**7:11**	**5:3**
___	___	___
3:2	**4:15**	**1:1**
___	___	___
3:5	**7:4**	**2:3**
___	___	___
2:1	**15:13**	**4:5**

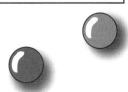

UNIT 9

Name: _____   Date: _____

NCTM Standard: Number and Operations – understand ways of representing numbers and work flexibly with positive and negative numbers

Conquer Positive and Negative Numbers

+19.5 ___	**+4.75** ___	**0** ___
+1 ___	**-6** ___	**+3.25** ___
-5 ___	**-4** ___	**-3** ___
-4.5 ___	**+5** ___	**-1.5** ___
-19.5 ___	**-2** ___	**+0.5** ___

The arrow on the line between each set of numbers represents a whole number and/or a decimal part of the line. Find the whole number or decimal represented by the arrow in the boxes above. Write the item number on the line in the box that has the correct answer.

1.   -2 ⟶↑⟶ +2   **2.**   0 ⟶↑⟶ +2

3.   -2 ⟶↑⟶ -1   **4.**   -3 ⟶↑⟶ -1

5.   -5 ⟶↑⟶ -4   **6.**   -5 ⟶↑⟶ -3

7.   +3 ⟶↑⟶ +4   **8.**   +4 ⟶↑⟶ +6

9.   -6 ⟶↑⟶ -4   **10.**   +4 ⟶↑⟶ +5

11.   -7 ⟶↑⟶ -5   **12.**   -6 ⟶↑⟶ -2

13.   -20 ⟶↑⟶ -19   **14.**   +19 ⟶↑⟶ +20

15.   0 ⟶↑⟶ +1

Name: _____   Date: _____

NCTM Standard: Number and Operations – understand relationships among numbers

Mark Some Positive and Negative Numbers

-3 ___	**-15** ___	**-19** ___
4 ___	**5** ___	**-16** ___
-18 ___	**-1** ___	**-10** ___
-14 ___	**-5** ___	**-9** ___
-2 ___	**0** ___	**-8** ___

Determine the number represented by the arrow on each number line. Find the answers in the boxes above. Write the item number on the line in the box that has the correct answer.

1. -2 ——————↑—————— 0
2. -19 ——————↑—————— -17
3. -20 ——————↑—————— -18
4. -4 ——————↑—————— 0
5. -21 ——————↑—————— -11
6. -15 ——————↑—————— -13
7. -11 ——————↑—————— -7
8. -4 ——————↑—————— -2
9. -9 ——————↑—————— -1
10. 3 ——————↑—————— 5
11. 2 ——————↑—————— 8
12. -10 ——————↑—————— -6
13. -20 ——————↑—————— -10
14. -15 ——————↑—————— -5
15. -6 ——————↑—————— 6

Name: _____   Date: _____

NCTM Standard: Number and Operations – compute fluently and make reasonable estimates

Pocket Positive and Negative Solutions

+35 ___	+36 ___	-12 ___	-30 ___
-23 ___	-31 ___	-11 ___	-120 ___
-22 ___	-134 ___	0 ___	+33 ___
-96 ___	-59 ___	+20 ___	+11 ___

Find the solution to each of the addition problems below in the boxes above. Write the item number on the line in the box that has the correct answer.

1. -35 + -61 =   **2.** +56 + -23 =

3. +43 + -73 =   **4.** -45 + +22 =

5. +56 + -21 =   **6.** -102 + -32 =

7. +23 + -35 =   **8.** +34 + -56 =

9. +109 + -73 =   **10.** +21 + -10 =

11. +62 + -93 =   **12.** -38 + -21 =

13. -30 + -90 =   **14.** +21 + -21 =

15. -20 + +40 =   **16.** +32 + -43 =

Name: _____   Date: _____

NCTM Standard: Number and Operations – understand relationships among numbers

Hook Some Patterns

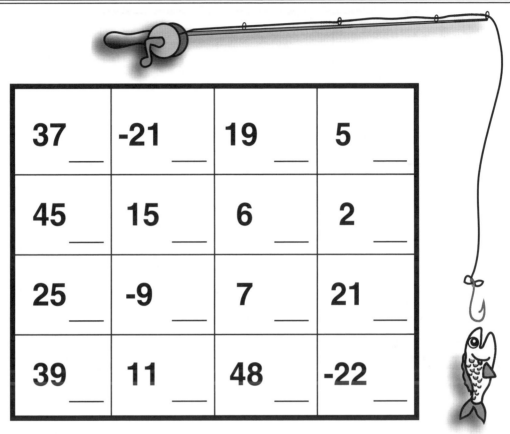

37 __	-21 __	19 __	5 __
45 __	15 __	6 __	2 __
25 __	-9 __	7 __	21 __
39 __	11 __	48 __	-22 __

Determine the number that comes next in each pattern below, and find the answer in the boxes above. Write the item number on the line in the box that has the correct answer.

1. 5, 10, 15, 20, _____

2. 3, 6, 9, 12, _____

3. 9, 8, 7, 6, _____

4. 32, 36, 40, 44, _____

5. 31, 33, 35, 37, _____

6. 35, 36, 38, 41, _____

7. 35, 39, 36, 40, _____

8. -1, -3, -5, -7, _____

9. -1, +2, +5, +8, _____

10. 3, 5, 4, 6, 5, _____

11. 33, 30, 27, 24, _____

12. 42, 33, 24, 15, _____

13. -7, -9, -12, -16, _____

14. -2, -7, -12, -17, _____

15. 5, 10, 14, 17, _____

16. 28, 20, 13, 7, _____

UNIT 11

Name: _____   Date: _____

NCTM Standard: Number and Operations – understand relationships among numbers

Pick Up a Numerical Pattern

621	-46	-529	5,900
5,560	-509	577	-36
559	-35	565	531
5,967	541	598	5,550

Determine the numerical pattern in each problem below. Then find the number that would come next in the pattern in the boxes above. Write the item number on the line in the box that has the correct answer.

1. 545; 550; 555; 560; …
2. 5,545; 5,550; 5,555; …
3. 5,565; 5,560; 5,555; …
4. 575; 571; 567; 563; …
5. 5,700; 5,750; 5,800; 5,850; …
6. 5,999; 5,991; 5,983; 5,975; …
7. 576; 567; 558; 549; 540; …
8. 576; 569; 562; 555; 548; …
9. -45; -43; -41; -39; -37; …
10. -31; -34; -37; -40; -43; …
11. -51; -46; -42; -39; -37; …
12. 521; 541; 561; 581; 601; …
13. 632; 621; 610; 599; 588; …
14. -521; -523; -525; -527; …
15. -521; -518; -515; -512; …
16. 568; 572; 577; 583; 590; …

22 27 32 37 42 47

UNIT 11

Name: _____ Date: _____

NCTM Standard: Algebra – use symbolic algebra to represent problems

Nab an Expression

___ $n + 6$	___ $n + 3$	___ $n \div 4$	___ $n - 6$
___ $5 \div n$	___ $15 \div n$	___ $6 - n$	___ $6n$
___ $n \div 6$	___ $6 + n$	___ $3 - n$	___ $n \div 5$
___ $5n$	___ $3 + n$	___ $3n$	___ $4 \div n$

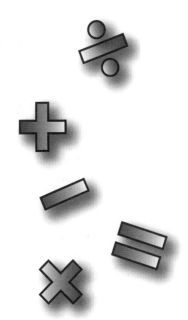

Match each algebraic expression below with an equation in the boxes above. Write the item number on the line in the box that has the correct answer.

1. *n* more than the quantity six
2. the quantity fifteen divided by *n*
3. six more than the quantity *n*
4. the quantity five divided by *n*
5. five times the quantity *n*
6. six less than *n*
7. *n* more than the quantity three
8. *n* less than the quantity six
9. the quantity *n* divided by five
10. the quantity *n* divided by four
11. *n* divided by the quantity six
12. six times the quantity *n*
13. *n* subtracted from the quantity three
14. four divided by the quantity *n*
15. three added to the quantity *n*
16. the quantity three times *n*

Name: _____ Date: _____

NCTM Standard: Algebra – use symbolic algebra to represent problems; represent the idea of an unknown in expressions and equations

Dance Away With Algebraic Expressions

—— six added to *n*	—— 5 minus the quantity *n*	—— the quantity *a* added to 6
—— *a* less than 5	—— 5 more than *a*	—— *n*, take away 6
—— 3 more than *n*	—— *a* taken away from 6	—— 4 more than *n*
—— *a* more than 5	—— 5 less than *n*	—— the quantity *n* added to 4
—— the quantity *n* added to 3	—— 6 added to *a*	—— *a* minus the quantity 6

Below are algebraic expressions. Find the definition of each expression in the boxes above. Write the item number on the line in the box that has the correct answer.

1. $a + 5 =$ **2.** $5 + a =$ **3.** $n + 4 =$

4. $n + 3 =$ **5.** $a + 6 =$ **6.** $n + 6 =$

7. $4 + n =$ **8.** $3 + n =$ **9.** $6 + a =$

10. $n - 5 =$ **11.** $5 - a =$ **12.** $6 - a =$

13. $n - 6 =$ **14.** $a - 6 =$ **15.** $5 - n =$

Name: _____ Date: _____

NCTM Standard: Algebra – use symbolic algebra to represent problems

Peg Some Algebraic Equations

11 __	10 __	12 __	90 __
4 __	14 __	2 __	94 __
8 __	5 __	3 __	70 __
9 __	7 __	25 __	6 __

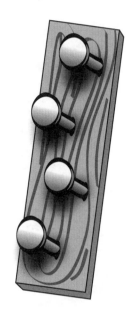

Decide the value of the unknown factor or divisor in each equation below, and find the answer in the boxes above. Write the item number on the line in the box that has the correct answer.

1. $55 \div n = 5$
2. $22 \times n = 88$
3. $34 \times n = 68$
4. $78 \div n = 26$
5. $96 \div n = 12$
6. $72 \div n = 6$
7. $24 \times n = 144$
8. $20 \times n = 280$
9. $27 \times n = 189$
10. $32 \times n = 160$
11. $234 \div n = 26$
12. $500 \div n = 50$
13. $420 \div n = 6$
14. $540 \div n = 6$
15. $2 \times n = 188$
16. $3 \times n = 75$

Name: _____ Date: _____

NCTM Standard: Number and Operations – compute fluently and make reasonable estimates

Glide Through Algebraic Equations

12 __	0.8 __	40 __	10 __
2 __	30 __	50 __	5 __
0.6 __	6 __	20 __	7 __
3 __	0.1 __	0.7 __	9 __

Solve the equations below, and find the value for the unknown in the boxes above. Write the item number on the line in the box that has the correct answer.

1. $0.369 \div n = 0.123$
2. $0.205 \div a = 0.041$
3. $0.50 \div y = 0.05$
4. $0.568 \div n = 0.71$
5. $0.639 \div y = 0.071$
6. $0.357 \div n = 0.51$
7. $0.306 \div a = 0.051$
8. $0.546 \div m = 0.91$
9. $0.637 \div n = 0.091$
10. $0.526 \div y = 0.263$
11. $0.789 \div n = 0.0263$
12. $0.32 \div m = 0.016$
13. $0.50 \div n = 5$
14. $0.60 \div y = 0.05$
15. $0.160 \div m = 0.004$
16. $0.250 \div a = 0.005$

Name: _____ Date: _____

NCTM Standard: Algebra – use symbolic algebra to represent problems; determine value of unknown in expressions and equations

Hook Algebraic Unknowns

___ $m = 1$	___ $n = 10$	___ $p = 3$	___ $m = 2$
___ $p = 12$	___ $a = 30$	___ $a = 3$	___ $m = 9$
___ $a = 12$	___ $p = 4$	___ $n = 5$	___ $p = 8$
___ $n = 3$	___ $n = 6$	___ $m = 5$	___ $a = 7$

Solve the equations below by finding the value of the unknown. Then find the answer in the boxes above. Write the item number on the line in the box that has the correct answer.

1. $45 = 5n - 5$

2. $15 = 2a + 9$

3. $13 = 3p + 1$

4. $16 = 3m + 1$

5. $18 = 5n + 3$

6. $38 = 3p + 2$

7. $65 = 5a + 5$

8. $37 = 4m + 1$

9. $12 = 2n + 2$

10. $32 = 4a + 4$

11. $29 = 5p - 11$

12. $25 = 3m + 19$

13. $27 = 4n + 3$

14. $92 = 3a + 2$

15. $23 = 4p + 11$

16. $9 = 5m + 4$

Name: _____   Date: _____

NCTM Standard: Algebra – represent mathematical situations using algebraic symbols

Zip Away With Algebraic Expressions

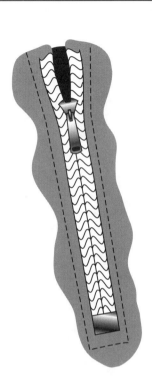

$n/4$	$a + 5$	$y - 4$	$6 + a$
$n + 5$	$n + 12$	$12/a$	$n - 6$
$y - 6$	$n - 3$	$4/n$	$a - 6$
$n - 5$	$4 - n$	$n + 4$	$z + 6$

Read each description below, and find the matching expression in the boxes above. Write the item number on the line in the box that has the correct answer.

1. 5 more than the quantity a
2. 3 less than the quantity n
3. 6 added to the quantity z
4. 5 less than the quantity n
5. 6 less than the quantity n
6. 5 more than the quantity n
7. n less than 4
8. 4 divided by the quantity n
9. the quantity n divided by 4
10. 6 less than the quantity a
11. the quantity a more than 6
12. 12 more than the quantity n
13. 12 divided by the quantity a
14. 6 less than the quantity y
15. the quantity n plus 4
16. the quantity y minus 4

UNIT 11

Name: _____ Date: _____

NCTM Standard: Number and Operations – identify and use relationships between operations, such as the commutative property

Button Down the Commutative Property

⎯⎯⎯ 22 x 15 x 16 =	⎯⎯⎯ 16 + 13 + 17 =	⎯⎯⎯ 31 x 15 x 22 =
⎯⎯⎯ 20 + 23 + 22 =	⎯⎯⎯ 20 x 21 x 22 =	⎯⎯⎯ 27 + 20 + 21 =
⎯⎯⎯ 22 + 27 + 25 =	⎯⎯⎯ 12 + 13 + 15 =	⎯⎯⎯ 26 + 25 + 20 =
⎯⎯⎯ 12 + 16 + 20 =	⎯⎯⎯ 20 + 27 + 22 =	⎯⎯⎯ 25 x 15 x 23 =
⎯⎯⎯ 25 x 22 x 30 =	⎯⎯⎯ 16 + 14 + 20 =	⎯⎯⎯ 26 x 20 x 25 =

For each problem below, find the corresponding problem that shows the commutative property in the boxes above. Write the item number on the line in the box that has the correct answer.

1. 14 + 16 + 20 =

2. 22 x 16 x 15 =

3. 13 + 17 + 16 =

4. 23 x 25 x 15 =

5. 20 x 22 x 21 =

6. 20 + 25 + 26 =

7. 20 + 22 + 27 =

8. 23 + 22 + 20 =

9. 25 + 22 + 27 =

10. 15 x 22 x 31 =

11. 13 + 12 + 15 =

12. 25 x 26 x 20 =

13. 20 + 21 + 27 =

14. 16 + 20 + 12 =

15. 30 x 25 x 22 =

Name: _____ Date: _____

NCTM Standard: Number and Operations – understand and use properties of operations such as the distributivity of multiplication over addition

Draw in the Distributive Property

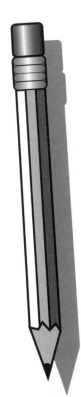

____	____	____
(6 x 40) + (6 x 5)	**(8 x 50) + (8 x 3)**	**(7 x 50) + (7 x 4)**
____	____	____
(8 x 30) + (8 x 5)	**(6 x 50) + (6 x 7)**	**(7 x 50) + (7 x 7)**
____	____	____
(8 x 50) + (8 x 4)	**(7 x 40) + (7 x 5)**	**(7 x 70) + (7 x 5)**
____	____	____
(7 x 30) + (7 x 5)	**(5 x 80) + (5 x 4)**	**(6 x 70) + (6 x 5)**
____	____	____
(8 x 40) + (8 x 5)	**(5 x 40) + (5 x 8)**	**(6 x 50) + (6 x 4)**

Below are some multiplication problems. Find the easier solution to each problem showing the use of the distributive property in the boxes above. Write the item number on the line in the box that has the correct answer.

1. 8 x 45 =   **2.** 6 x 57 =   **3.** 6 x 75 =

4. 8 x 54 =   **5.** 5 x 84 =   **6.** 6 x 54 =

7. 7 x 75 =   **8.** 5 x 48 =   **9.** 6 x 45 =

10. 7 x 57 =   **11.** 8 x 35 =   **12.** 7 x 54 =

13. 8 x 53 =   **14.** 7 x 35 =   **15.** 7 x 45 =

Name: _____ Date: _____

NCTM Standard: Number and Operations – understand relationships among numbers

Douse the Density Property

____ $3\frac{3}{12}$ or $3\frac{1}{4}$	____ $2\frac{9}{18}$ or $2\frac{1}{2}$	____ $1\frac{7}{10}$
____ $\frac{3}{10}$	____ $\frac{11}{18}$	____ $\frac{3}{18}$ or $\frac{1}{6}$
____ $5\frac{3}{14}$	____ $\frac{3}{12}$ or $\frac{1}{4}$	____ $2\frac{3}{16}$
____ $1\frac{3}{8}$	____ $\frac{3}{24}$ or $\frac{1}{8}$	____ $\frac{7}{14}$ or $\frac{1}{2}$
____ $3\frac{3}{6}$ or $3\frac{1}{2}$	____ $\frac{11}{16}$	____ $\frac{7}{10}$

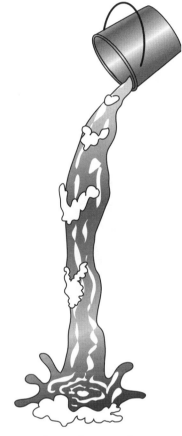

The density property states that "between every two rational numbers, no matter how close, there is another rational number." For each item below, find the rational number that would be between the two rational numbers. Write the item number on the line in the box that has the correct answer.

1. $\frac{1}{5}$ ↑ $\frac{2}{5}$
2. $\frac{1}{6}$ ↑ $\frac{2}{6}$
3. $\frac{3}{5}$ ↑ $\frac{4}{5}$
4. $2\frac{1}{8}$ ↑ $2\frac{2}{8}$
5. $3\frac{1}{3}$ ↑ $3\frac{2}{3}$
6. $1\frac{3}{5}$ ↑ $1\frac{4}{5}$
7. $5\frac{1}{7}$ ↑ $5\frac{2}{7}$
8. $\frac{5}{8}$ ↑ $\frac{6}{8}$
9. $\frac{3}{7}$ ↑ $\frac{4}{7}$
10. $\frac{5}{9}$ ↑ $\frac{6}{9}$
11. $\frac{1}{12}$ ↑ $\frac{2}{12}$
12. $1\frac{1}{4}$ ↑ $1\frac{1}{2}$
13. $\frac{1}{9}$ ↑ $\frac{2}{9}$
14. $3\frac{1}{6}$ ↑ $3\frac{2}{6}$
15. $2\frac{4}{9}$ ↑ $2\frac{5}{9}$

Name: _____ Date: _____

NCTM Standard: Number and Operations – understand ways of representing numbers, use exponential notation

Overcome Exponents

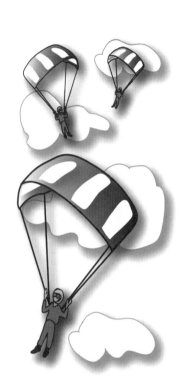

125 ___	4 ___	16 ___	121 ___
100 ___	8 ___	27 ___	25 ___
64 ___	256 ___	36 ___	32 ___
49 ___	9 ___	144 ___	81 ___

Find the values of the numbers with exponents below in the boxes above. Write the item number on the line in the box that has the correct answer.

1. 2^2	**2.** 3^2	**3.** 4^2	**4.** 5^2
5. 6^2	**6.** 10^2	**7.** 8^2	**8.** 7^2
9. 9^2	**10.** 3^3	**11.** 4^4	**12.** 11^2
13. 2^3	**14.** 5^3	**15.** 12^2	**16.** 2^5

Name: _____ Date: _____

NCTM Standard: Number and Operations – compute fluently and make reasonable estimates

Latch on to Square Root Estimations

____ **25**	____ **between 12 and 13**	____ **between 5 and 6**
____ **between 3 and 4**	____ **between 1 and 2**	____ **between 14 and 15**
____ **between 8 and 9**	____ **between 15 and 16**	____ **between 7 and 8**
____ **between 13 and 14**	____ **between 4 and 5**	____ **20**
____ **between 11 and 12**	**30**	____ **between 9 and 10**

For each number below, find the exact square root or a reasonable range of the square root in the boxes above. Write the item number on the line in the box that has the correct answer.

1. 26	**2.** 250	**3.** 17	**4.** 68
5. 85	**6.** 150	**7.** 50	**8.** 10
9. 3	**10.** 125	**11.** 180	**12.** 200
13. 400	**14.** 625	**15.** 900	

Name: _____   Date: _____

NCTM Standard: Number and Operations – understand ways of representing numbers; make reasonable estimates

Search for a Square Root

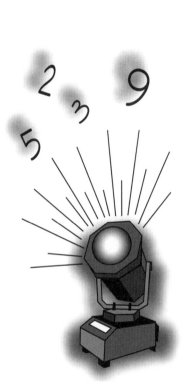

3.46 ___	5.10 ___	11 ___
5 ___	8.2 ___	12 ___
8.06 ___	11.8 ___	8 ___
10.9 ___	3 ___	2.8 ___
5.3 ___	5.9 ___	12.17 ___

Find the square root of each number below. The answers have been rounded and are in the boxes above. Write the item number on the line in the box that has the correct answer.

1. 144	**2.** 140	**3.** 35	**4.** 68
5. 64	**6.** 28	**7.** 9	**8.** 8
9. 26	**10.** 65	**11.** 119	**12.** 25
13. 148	**14.** 121	**15.** 12	

Name: _____ Date: _____

NCTM Standard: Number and Operations – make reasonable estimates

Strike Out Square Roots

8 ___	7.874 ___	3.873 ___
8.426 ___	6.164 ___	3.6 ___
5.916 ___	10 ___	6.7 ___
5.385 ___	7 ___	9.22 ___
8.718 ___	7.416 ___	9 ___

If the square root of 25 is 5 and the square root of 36 is 6, then the square root of 26 is somewhere between 5 and 6. Estimate which square root in the boxes above would be at the place of the arrow for each item below. Write the item number on the line in the box that has the correct answer.

1. 28 ↑ 30

2. 36 ↑ 40

3. 40 ↑ 50

4. 50 ↑ 60

5. 60 ↑ 64

6. 70 ↑ 72

7. 75 ↑ 77

8. 34 ↑ 36

9. 48 ↑ 50

10. 60 ↑ 68

11. 78 ↑ 84

12. 98 ↑ 102

13. 80 ↑ 90

14. 10 ↑ 20

15. 12 ↑ 14

Name: _____   Date: _____

NCTM Standard: Number and Operations – understand proportions and represent quantitative relationships

Pounce on Proportions

$n = 28$ ___	$n = 0.5$ ___	$n = 25$ ___
$n = 5$ ___	$n = 24$ ___	$n = 13.5$ ___
$n = 1.6$ ___	$n = 9.375$ ___	$n = 10$ ___
$n = 2.08\overline{3}$ ___	$n = 4$ ___	$n = 30$ ___
$n = 3.2$ ___	$n = 2$ ___	$n = 3$ ___

Below are a number of proportions. Solve these by cross-multiplying, and then find the correct answer for each in the boxes above. Write the item number on the line in the box that has the correct answer.

1. $\dfrac{1}{2} = \dfrac{n}{6}$ 2. $\dfrac{5}{8} = \dfrac{n}{15}$ 3. $\dfrac{5}{7} = \dfrac{20}{n}$

4. $\dfrac{n}{4} = \dfrac{16}{20}$ 5. $\dfrac{10}{n} = \dfrac{15}{45}$ 6. $\dfrac{5}{n} = \dfrac{12}{5}$

7. $\dfrac{8}{9} = \dfrac{12}{n}$ 8. $\dfrac{3}{n} = \dfrac{24}{4}$ 9. $\dfrac{n}{9} = \dfrac{15}{27}$

10. $\dfrac{4}{n} = \dfrac{16}{8}$ 11. $\dfrac{n}{5} = \dfrac{30}{6}$ 12. $\dfrac{6}{n} = \dfrac{30}{8}$

13. $\dfrac{5}{n} = \dfrac{25}{20}$ 14. $\dfrac{n}{6} = \dfrac{28}{7}$ 15. $\dfrac{8}{12} = \dfrac{n}{15}$

UNIT 13

Name: _____   Date: _____

NCTM Standard: Measurement – understand both metric and customary systems of measurement

Crunch Customary Units

Use the inch ruler directly below to measure each of the long boxes beneath it, and then find the answer in the boxes to the right. Write the item number on the line in the box that has the correct answer.

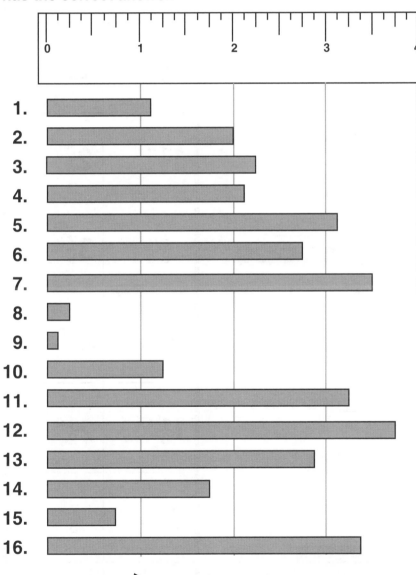

$3\frac{3}{4}''$ ___	$2\frac{1}{4}''$ ___
$3\frac{3}{8}''$ ___	$\frac{1}{8}''$ ___
$3\frac{1}{2}''$ ___	$1\frac{3}{4}''$ ___
$1\frac{1}{4}''$ ___	$1\frac{1}{8}''$ ___
$\frac{1}{4}''$ ___	$2''$ ___
$\frac{3}{4}''$ ___	$3\frac{1}{8}''$ ___
$2\frac{1}{8}''$ ___	$2\frac{7}{8}''$ ___
$2\frac{3}{4}''$ ___	$3\frac{1}{4}''$ ___

1.
2.
3.
4.
5.
6.
7.
8.
9.
10.
11.
12.
13.
14.
15.
16.

UNIT 14

Name: _____ Date: _____

NCTM Standard: Measurement – understand both metric and customary systems of measurement

Swap Customary Units

Use the inch ruler directly below to measure each of the long boxes beneath it, and then find the answer in the boxes to the right. Write the item number on the line in the box that has the correct answer.

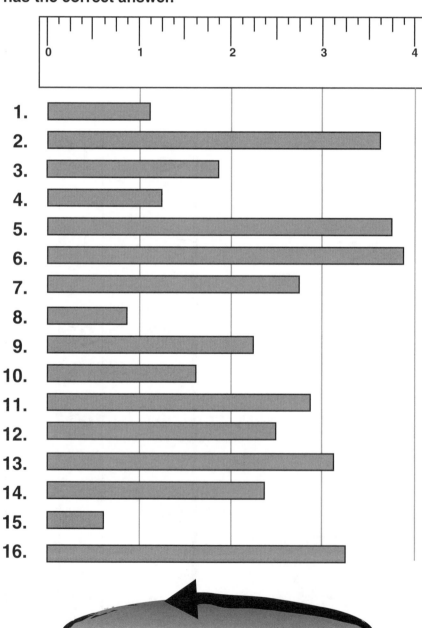

$2\frac{7}{8}''$ ___	$3\frac{1}{4}''$ ___
$1\frac{7}{8}''$ ___	$2\frac{1}{4}''$ ___
$1\frac{1}{4}''$ ___	$2\frac{3}{4}''$ ___
$\frac{5}{8}''$ ___	$3\frac{7}{8}''$ ___
$1\frac{5}{8}''$ ___	$2\frac{3}{8}''$ ___
$1\frac{1}{8}''$ ___	$2\frac{1}{2}''$ ___
$3\frac{5}{8}''$ ___	$\frac{7}{8}''$ ___
$3\frac{1}{8}''$ ___	$3\frac{3}{4}''$ ___

UNIT 14

Name: _____ Date: _____

NCTM Standard: Measurement – understand both metric and customary systems of measurement

Tackle Metric Measurement

The ruler directly below *represents* metric measurement. Use it to measure each of the long boxes beneath it, and then find the answer in the boxes to the right. Write the item number on the line in the box that has the correct answer.

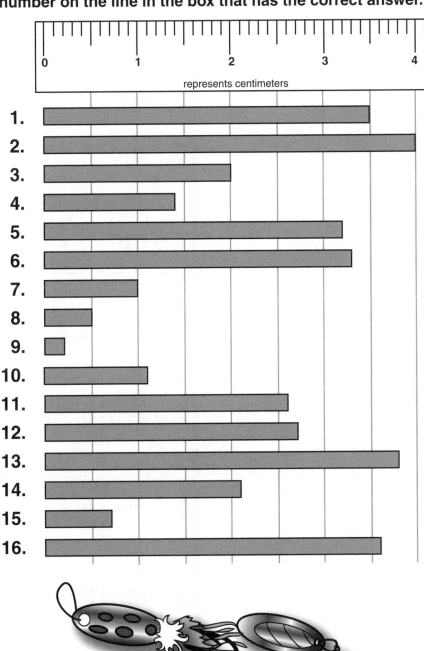

represents centimeters

3.8 cm ——	2.1 cm ——
2.0 cm ——	3.2 cm ——
3.3 cm ——	0.5 cm ——
1.1 cm ——	1.4 cm ——
3.6 cm ——	3.5 cm ——
2.7 cm ——	1.0 cm ——
2.6 cm ——	0.7 cm ——
4.0 cm ——	0.2 cm ——

UNIT 14

Name: _____ Date: _____

NCTM Standard: Measurement – understand both metric and customary systems of measurement

Munch Some Metrics

The ruler directly below *represents* metric measurement. Use it to measure each of the long boxes beneath it, and then find the answer in the boxes to the right. Write the item number on the line in the box that has the correct answer.

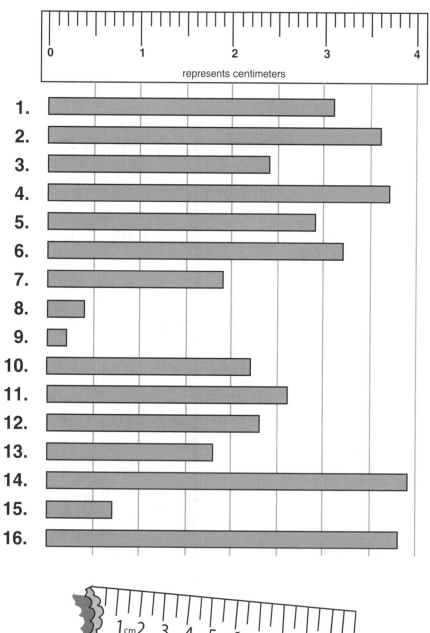

2.2 cm	3.9 cm
——	——
0.4 cm	1.9 cm
——	——
3.7 cm	1.8 cm
——	——
2.6 cm	3.1 cm
——	——
2.3 cm	3.2 cm
——	——
2.9 cm	0.7 cm
——	——
3.6 cm	0.2 cm
——	——
3.8 cm	2.4 cm
——	——

Name: _____   Date: _____

NCTM Standard: Geometry – analyze properties of two-dimensional shapes or objects

Lasso Lines and Points

angle ___	pro-tractor ___	acute angle ___	parallel lines ___
straight angle ___	point ___	comple-mentary angles ___	line segment ___
perpen-dicular lines ___	curve ___	angle bisector ___	obtuse angle ___
ray ___	skew lines ___	vertex ___	supple-mentary angles ___

Read the definitions below, and find the corresponding answer in the boxes above. Write the item number on the line in the box that has the correct answer.

The name:

1. of an exact location
2. of a piece of a line with 2 endpoints
3. of two lines that are an exact distance apart and that never meet
4. of two lines that are in different planes and are neither parallel nor intersecting
5. of two lines that meet and form right angles
6. of a line that bends and can form an opened or closed figure
7. of a line that goes in one direction without stopping and has one endpoint

8. of two rays that have a common endpoint
9. of an angle that measures 180°
10. of two angles that add up to 180°
11. of two angles that together add up to 90°
12. of a ray that separates an angle into two congruent angles
13. of the tool used to measure angles
14. of the point of an angle
15. of an angle that is less than 90°
16. of an angle that is more than 90°

Name: _____ Date: _____

NCTM Standard: Geometry – analyze properties of two-dimensional shapes

Search for the Geometric Gold

isosceles ___	comple- mentary angles ___	triangle ___	supple- mentary angles ___
trapezoid ___	square ___	interior angle ___	right triangle ___
equi- lateral triangle ___	scalene ___	parallel lines ___	parallelo- gram ___
rhombus ___	obtuse angle ___	point ___	rectangle ___

Match the definitions below with the answers in the boxes above. Write the item number on the line in the box that has the correct answer.

1. A shape with 4 congruent sides and 4 right angles
2. A shape with 4 sides, with the opposite sides parallel and equal
3. A shape with 3 sides
4. A specific place in space
5. A shape with 3 congruent sides
6. Lines in the same plane that never cross
7. An angle inside of a polygon
8. A shape with 2 pairs of parallel lines and 4 congruent sides
9. A triangle with 2 congruent sides
10. A triangle with no congruent sides

11. A quadrilateral with one pair of parallel lines
12. A shape with 2 pairs of parallel lines, 4 right angles, and 2 pairs of congruent sides
13. A triangle with one 90° angle
14. An angle larger than 90°
15. When 2 angles add up to 90°
16. When the sum of 2 angles is 180°

Name: _____   Date: _____

NCTM Standard: Geometry – describe, classify, and understand relationships among two-dimensional objects; understand relations between angles, side lengths, perimeters, and areas; apply the correct formula to solve a problem

Play With Perimeters

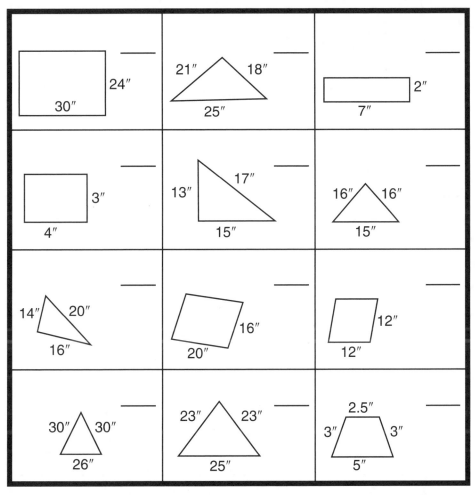

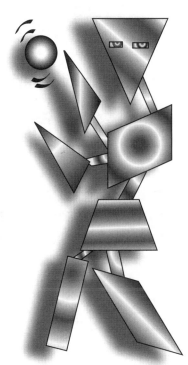

Match each perimeter below with the corresponding geometric shape having that perimeter in the boxes above. Write the item number on the line in the box that has the correct answer.

1. 45 inches   2. 13.5 inches   3. 14 inches

4. 18 inches   5. 86 inches   6. 50 inches

7. 47 inches   8. 64 inches   9. 71 inches

10. 108 inches   11. 72 inches   12. 48 inches

Name: _____ Date: _____

NCTM Standard: Geometry – understand relationships among two-dimensional objects, using defining properties such as perimeter, area, surface area, and volume

Buffalo Some Triangular Perimeters

Determine the perimeter of each triangle in the boxes to the left. Match the perimeters below with the correct triangles to the left. Write the item number on the line in the box that has the correct answer.

1.   32 inches
2.   12.8 inches
3.   27.4 inches
4.   29.3 inches
5.   23.4 inches
6.   49.5 inches
7.   43 inches
8.   18.8 inches
9.   15.7 inches
10. 18.2 inches
11. 17.9 inches
12. 15.2 inches
13. 44.5 inches
14. 24 inches
15. 20.9 inches

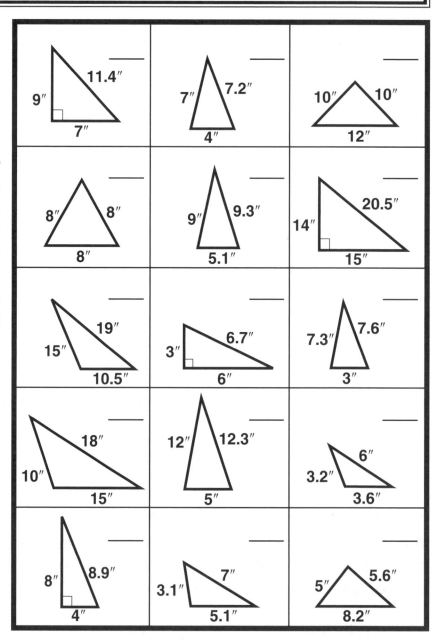

CD-404152 © Mark Twain Media, Inc., Publishers

Name: _____ Date: _____

NCTM Standard: Geometry – describe, classify, and understand relationships among two-dimensional objects; understand relations between angles, side lengths, perimeters, and areas; apply the correct formula to solve a problem

Reach for Rectangular Areas

5″ x 8″ ___	12″ x 10″ ___	18′ x 2′ ___
64′ x 2′ ___	5′ x 10′ ___	52′ x 2′ ___
25′ x 5′ ___	20″ x 3″ ___	21′ x 4′ ___
14″ x 3″ ___	15′ x 3′ ___	11″ x 8″ ___
13′ x 5′ ___	12″ x 8″ ___	16′ x 10′ ___

Match each area below with the corresponding dimensions in the boxes above. Write the item number on the line in the box that has the correct answer.

1. 160 ft.^{2}	**2.** 50 ft.^{2}	**3.** 60 in.^{2}
4. 40 in.^{2}	**5.** 36 ft.^{2}	**6.** 45 ft.^{2}
7. 128 ft.^{2}	**8.** 120 in.^{2}	**9.** 42 in.^{2}
10. 125 ft.^{2}	**11.** 84 ft.^{2}	**12.** 65 ft.^{2}
13. 96 in.^{2}	**14.** 88 in.^{2}	**15.** 104 ft.^{2}

Name: _____ Date: _____

NCTM Standard: Geometry – identify, classify, and understand relationships among two-dimensional objects; understand relations between angles, side lengths, perimeters, and areas; apply the correct formula to solve a problem

Latch on to Areas

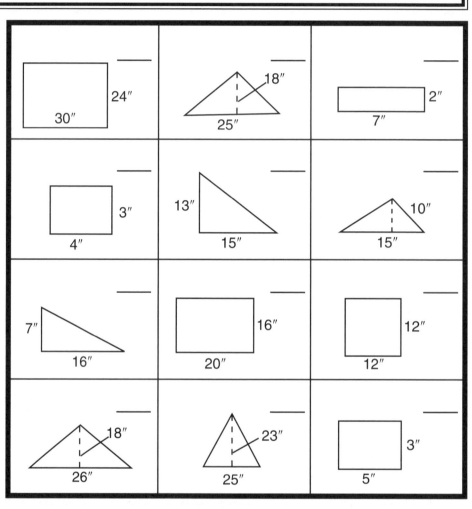

Match each area below with the corresponding geometric shape having that area in the boxes above. Write the item number on the line in the box that has the correct answer.

1. 144 square inches
2. 12 square inches
3. 15 square inches
4. 97.5 square inches
5. 287.5 square inches
6. 225 square inches
7. 320 square inches
8. 720 square inches
9. 75 square inches
10. 56 square inches
11. 14 square inches
12. 234 square inches

UNIT 15

Name: _____   Date: _____

NCTM Standard: Geometry – analyze properties of two-dimensional geometric shapes; understand relationships among areas of shapes

Latch on to Two-Dimensional Areas

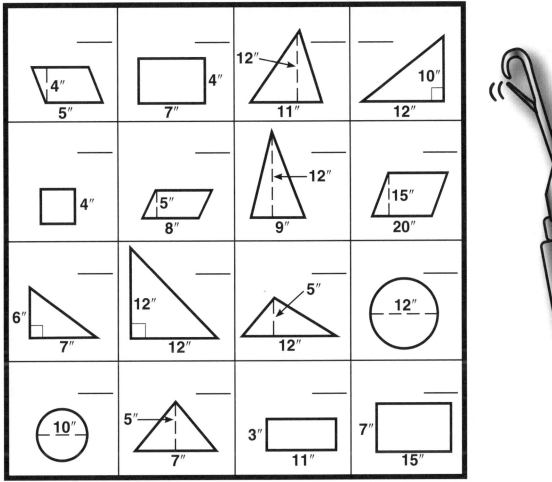

Find the areas of each of the shapes above. Then match the answers below to the shapes in the boxes above. Write the item number on the line in the box that has the correct answer.

1. 72 sq. inches
2. 78.5 sq. inches
3. 17.5 sq. inches
4. 105 sq. inches
5. 30 sq. inches
6. 66 sq. inches
7. 20 sq. inches
8. 40 sq. inches
9. 300 sq. inches
10. 28 sq. inches
11. 113.04 sq. inches
12. 54 sq. inches
13. 60 sq. inches
14. 16 sq. inches
15. 21 sq. inches
16. 33 sq. inches

Name: _____   Date: _____

NCTM Standard: Geometry – analyze properties of two-dimensional shapes;
Measurement – apply appropriate formulas to determine measurements

Crunch the Area of Triangles

—— 16 sq. in.	—— 22 sq. in.	—— 18 sq. in.	—— 32 sq. cm
—— 30 sq. in.	—— 24 sq. cm	—— 25 sq. cm	—— 15 sq. in.
—— 6 sq. in.	—— 12.5 sq. in.	—— 8 sq. cm	—— 27 sq. in.
—— 21 sq. in.	—— 10 sq. cm	—— 14 sq. in.	—— 20 sq. cm

Calculate each of the areas of triangles represented below and find the answer in the boxes above. Write the item number on the line in the box that has the correct answer.

	Length of Base	**Height**		**Length of Base**	**Height**
1.	12 cm	4 cm	**2.**	5 in.	6 in.
3.	4 cm	4 cm	**4.**	4 in.	8 in.
5.	5 cm	4 cm	**6.**	9 in.	4 in.
7.	10 cm	4 cm	**8.**	12 in.	5 in.
9.	7 in.	6 in.	**10.**	9 in.	6 in.
11.	8 cm	8 cm	**12.**	5 in.	5 in.
13.	6 in.	2 in.	**14.**	7 in.	4 in.
15.	10 cm	5 cm	**16.**	11 in.	4 in.

UNIT 15

Name: _____ Date: _____

NCTM Standard: Geometry – understand relationships among two-dimensional objects; be able to calculate area, surface area, and volume

Dive Into Triangular Areas

Find the area of each triangle to the right. Match the areas below with the correct triangles in the boxes to the right. Write the item number on the line in the box that has the correct answer.

1. 20 square inches
2. 36 square inches
3. $10\frac{1}{2}$ square inches
4. 45 square inches
5. 225 square inches
6. 6 square inches
7. 60 square inches
8. $27\frac{1}{2}$ square inches
9. 12 square inches
10. 25 square inches
11. 30 square inches
12. 75 square inches
13. 14 square inches
14. 375 square inches
15. 450 square inches

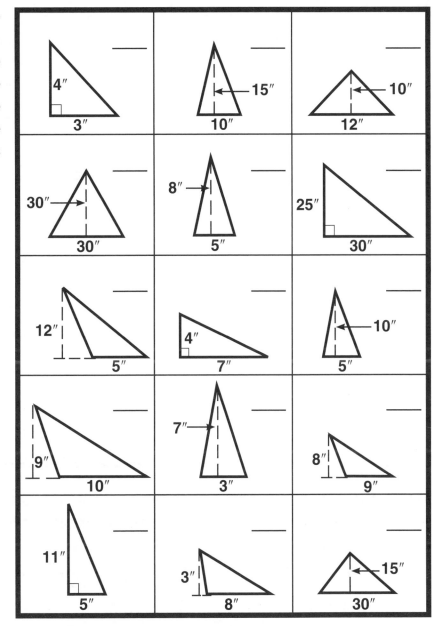

UNIT 15

Name: _____ Date: _____

NCTM Standard: Geometry – identify geometric figures

Conquer Geometric Shapes

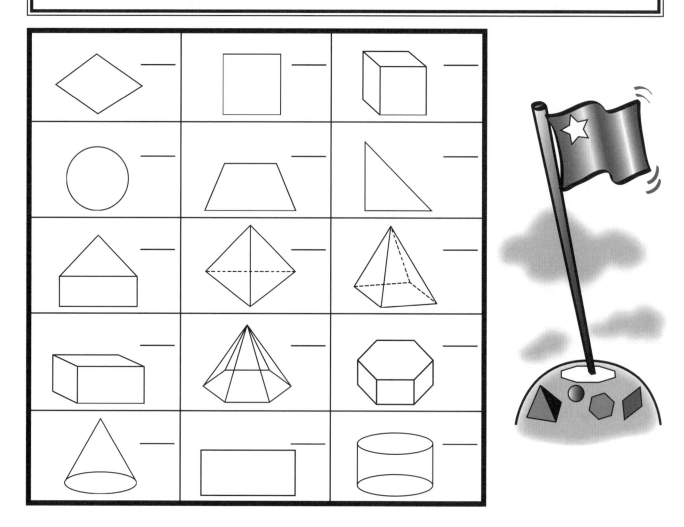

Match the name of each figure below with its corresponding geometric shape in the boxes above. Write the item number on the line in the box that has the correct answer.

1. cone	**2.** square pyramid	**3.** rhombus
4. trapezoid	**5.** circle	**6.** rectangular prism
7. triangular pyramid	**8.** rectangle	**9.** triangle
10. hexagonal prism	**11.** hexagonal pyramid	**12.** cube
13. square	**14.** triangular prism	**15.** cylinder

Name: _____ Date: _____

NCTM Standard: Geometry – understand relations between angles, side lengths, perimeters, surface areas, and volumes

Stamp Out Surface Areas

Find the surface areas of the shapes below in the boxes to the right. Each face that is on the outside of the shapes equals one square unit. Write the item number on the line in the box that has the correct answer.

$34 \ u^2$ ___	$48 \ u^2$ ___	$22 \ u^2$ ___
$18 \ u^2$ ___	$14 \ u^2$ ___	$40 \ u^2$ ___
$10 \ u^2$ ___	$46 \ u^2$ ___	$56 \ u^2$ ___
$6 \ u^2$ ___	$72 \ u^2$ ___	$26 \ u^2$ ___
$42 \ u^2$ ___	$30 \ u^2$ ___	$38 \ u^2$ ___

1.
2.
3.
4.
5.
6.
7.
8.
9.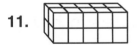
10.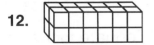
11.
12.
13.
14.
15.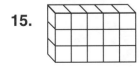

UNIT 15

Name: _____ Date: _____

NCTM Standard: Geometry – describe, classify, and understand relationships among two- and three-dimensional objects, using defining properties such as surface area and volume

Wangle Surface Areas

Find the surface area of each figure in the boxes below, and then match the surface areas to the right with the correct figures in the boxes. Write the item number on the line in the box that has the correct answer.

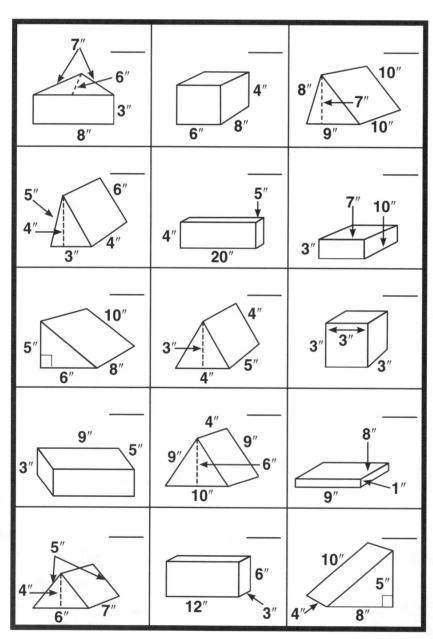

1. 132 square inches

2. 242 square inches

3. 198 square inches

4. 136 square inches

5. 208 square inches

6. 54 square inches

7. 400 square inches

8. 252 square inches

9. 72 square inches

10. 114 square inches

11. 333 square inches

12. 178 square inches

13. 68 square inches

14. 174 square inches

15. 172 square inches

Name: _____ Date: _____

NCTM Standard: Geometry – describe, classify, and understand relationships among two- and three-dimensional objects, using defining properties such as surface area and volume

Volley for Volume

Determine the volume for each figure in the boxes to the right, and then match the volumes below to the correct figures in the boxes. Write the item number on the line in the box that has the correct answer.

1. 90 cubic inches
2. 108 cubic inches
3. 2,250 cubic inches
4. 36 cubic inches
5. 140 cubic inches
6. 300 cubic inches
7. 30 cubic inches
8. 240 cubic inches
9. 144 cubic inches
10. 64 cubic inches
11. 440 cubic inches
12. 84 cubic inches
13. 200 cubic inches
14. 288 cubic inches
15. 168 cubic inches

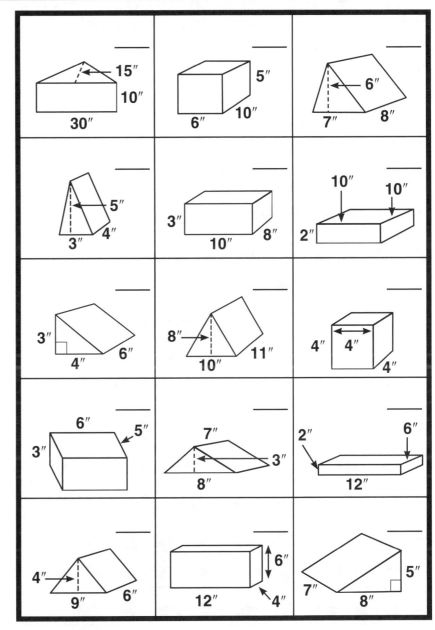

UNIT 15

Name: _____   Date: _____

NCTM Standard: Algebra – understand patterns; **Geometry** – apply transformations

Snatch Geometric Patterns

Complete each geometric pattern below with the correct shape in the boxes to the right. Write the item number on the line in the box that has the correct answer.

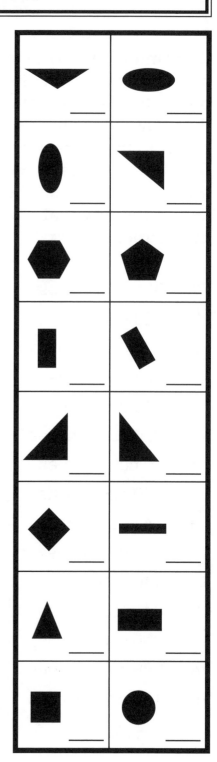

1.
2.
3.
4.
5.
6.
7.
8.
9.
10.
11.
12.
13.
14.
15.
16.

Name: _____ Date: _____

NCTM Standard: Geometry – analyze properties of two-dimensional geometric shapes; understand transformations

Grapple Geometric Patterns

In each item below is a series of geometric shapes. Find the next shape that would be in each pattern from the shapes in the boxes at the right. Write the item number on the line in the box that has the correct answer.

1. _____
2. _____
3. _____
4. _____
5. _____
6. _____
7. _____
8. _____
9. _____
10. _____
11. _____
12. _____
13. _____
14. _____
15. _____
16. _____

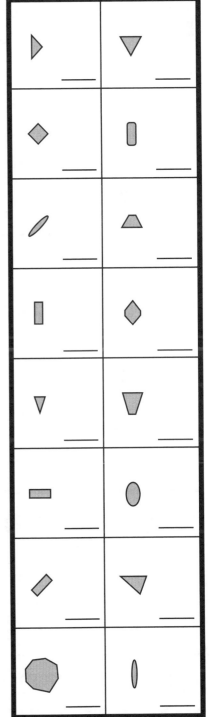

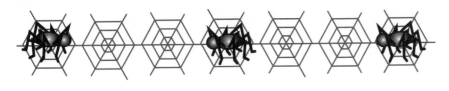

Name: _____ Date: _____

NCTM Standard: Geometry – specify locations using coordinate geometry

Master Coordinates

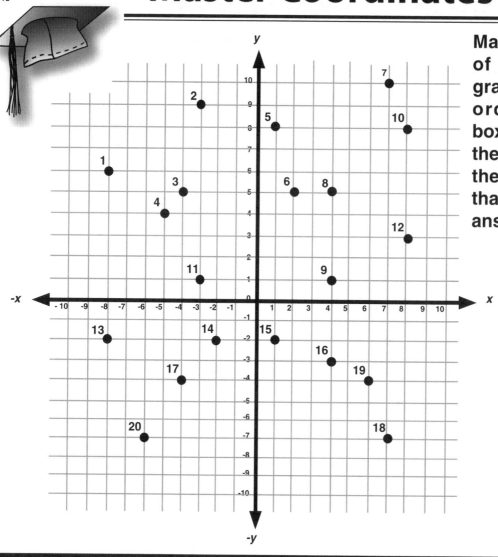

Match the number of the dot on the graph with the co-ordinates in the boxes below. Write the item number on the line in the box that has the correct answer.

(1,8) ___	(-8,-2) ___	(1,-2) ___	(-3,1) ___	(6,-4) ___
(-5,4) ___	(2,5) ___	(-2,-2) ___	(-8,6) ___	(4,-3) ___
(-3,9) ___	(-4,-4) ___	(-4,5) ___	(4,5) ___	(7,10) ___
(-6,-7) ___	(8,8) ___	(4,1) ___	(8,3) ___	(7,-7) ___

114

UNIT 15

Name: _____   Date: _____

NCTM Standard: Geometry – specify locations using coordinate geometry

Grab a Coordinate

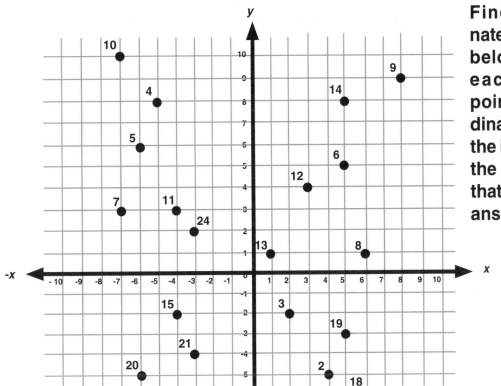

Find the coordinates in the boxes below that match each numbered point in the coordinate graph. Write the item number on the line in the box that has the correct answer.

(3,4) __	(5,-3) __	(2,-2) __	(5,8) __	(1,-8) __	(4,-5) __
(-4,-7) __	(5,5) __	(-7,3) __	(6,-6) __	(-4,3) __	(-3,-9) __
(8,-8) __	(1,1) __	(-6,-5) __	(-4,-2) __	(-5,8) __	(-3,2) __
(-7,10) __	(-5,-9) __	(-3,-4) __	(8,9) __	(-6,6) __	(6,1) __

UNIT 15

Name: _____ Date: _____

NCTM Standard: Data Analysis and Probability – formulate questions and analyze data; compute fluently and make reasonable estimates

Grip Some Graphing

Using the data on the graph, answer the questions below and find the answers in the boxes to the right. Write the item number on the line in the box that has the correct answer.

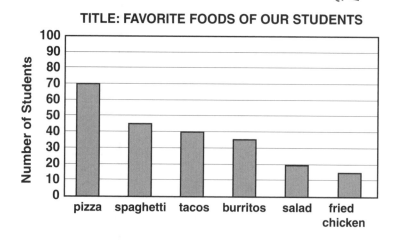

TITLE: FAVORITE FOODS OF OUR STUDENTS

1. What was the least favorite food of the school?
2. What was the favorite food?
3. How many students liked fried chicken?
4. How many more students liked pizza than spaghetti?
5. How many students were in this study?
6. How many students liked burritos and tacos?
7. What was the difference between the fried chicken and the pizza totals?
8. How many students preferred pizza, spaghetti, and tacos?
9. How many preferred burritos, salad, and fried chicken?
10. What percent of all the students liked pizza?
11. What percent of all the students liked fried chicken?
12. What percent of all the students like the top two choices?
13. What was the total number of students minus the total number of students who liked chicken?
14. What was the ratio of pizza students to taco students?
15. What was the ratio of salad students to taco students?

75 ___	7% ___	25 ___
225 ___	70:40 ___	31% ___
210 ___	chicken ___	55 ___
155 ___	70 ___	51% ___
15 ___	20:40 ___	pizza ___

UNIT 16

Name: _____   Date: _____

NCTM Standard: Data Analysis and Probability – analyze data and read various types of graphs

Lap Up Laps

Use the graph to answer the questions below, and find the answers in the boxes below. Write the item number on the line in the box that has the correct answer.

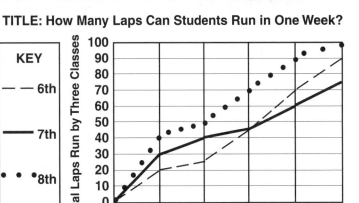

TITLE: How Many Laps Can Students Run in One Week?

1. If there were 20 students, how many laps did each seventh grader run on Monday?
2. Who ran the most laps in the five days?
3. Each class had 20 students. How many laps did each eighth grader run on Monday?
4. On Friday, how many laps did each eighth grader run?
5. On what day did the sixth and seventh graders run the same number of laps?
6. On what day were all the grades 10 laps apart?
7. On what day did the sixth grade make the least progress?
8. On Wednesday, what was the difference between the eighth graders and the other two classes?
9. On the last day, how many laps were run by all three classes?
10. What was the total laps run by all classes on Wednesday?
11. On Thursday, what was the difference in the laps of the sixth and seventh graders?
12. What class made a 45-lap increase in two consecutive days?
13. What was the increase in laps from Tuesday to Thursday for the eighth grade?
14. What class made the least progress from Tuesday to Wednesday?
15. How many laps did each seventh grader run on Friday?

___ 160 laps	___ 2 laps	___ 6th grade	___ 5 laps	___ 25 laps
___ $1\frac{1}{2}$ laps	___ 8th grade	___ 40 laps	___ Wednesday	___ 3.75 laps
___ Monday	___ 265 laps	___ Tuesday	___ 7th grade	___ 10 laps

UNIT 16

Answer Keys

*Only the problem numbers are included in the boxes. It is recommended to write the correct problem numbers on a full-size copy of each math game page to create an answer key.

Organize Ones, Tens, and Hundreds (p. 2)

5	12	7
13	1	10
3	8	2
6	4	14
11	15	9

Place Value Race (p. 3)

7	13	15
10	2	1
6	9	12
5	3	11
14	8	4

Bag Some Huge Numbers (p. 4)

1	12	4
10	3	15
5	14	6
11	2	13
7	9	8

Grab Base Ten Number Representations (p. 5)

11	4	13	6
2	1	12	7
16	10	3	15
8	9	14	5

Pull in Some Place Value (p. 6)

14	8	15
1	2	9
7	10	6
12	3	13
4	5	11

Ensnare Some Big Numbers (p. 7)

5	9	3	1
7	12	10	11
4	6	2	8

Roll in Tricky Place Value (p. 8)

3	10	4	13
9	6	15	7
12	2	8	16
1	14	5	11

Wangle Some Big Whole Numbers (p. 9)

8	5	16	9
15	1	12	6
2	10	4	13
7	14	3	11

Chalk Up a Sum (p. 10)

2	9	14	5
12	1	11	7
3	10	16	4
8	13	15	6

Catch the Sum (p. 11)

4	13	11	9
15	1	8	16
6	14	2	20
17	3	12	5
10	19	7	18

Grabbing *More Than* and *Less Than* Answers (p. 12)

10	9	1	6
13	5	14	8
7	15	2	12
3	11	16	4

Drag in Addition Estimation Answers (p. 13)

13	7	11
2	15	3
12	1	6
4	9	8
10	14	5

Rope Some Averages (p. 14)

6	16	2	12
7	1	11	8
4	13	3	14
10	9	15	5

Rescue Inverse Operations (p. 15)

7	13	1	10
11	2	8	16
3	9	14	5
6	12	4	15

Claim a Difference (p. 16)

5	14	7
6	1	15
12	4	11
3	9	2
13	8	10

Gain a Difference (p. 17)

4	5	12	1
14	2	16	15
10	13	7	9
6	11	3	8

Peg Subtraction Answers (p. 18)

1	9	14	8
7	13	4	12
11	2	10	5
6	16	3	15

Score With Multiples of *3* and *4* (p. 19)

18	7	6	15
1	10	20	4
16	5	14	11
3	13	2	12
17	9	8	19

Nab Multiples of *5* and *6* (p. 20)

1	16	10	13
18	6	8	19
3	11	17	2
15	7	9	20
14	12	5	4

Conquer Big Multiples (p. 21)

17	10	6	15
7	12	4	20
3	11	18	8
14	2	5	19
1	9	16	13

Snag a Big Multiple (p. 22)

2	4	6	8
15	12	1	5
7	11	16	10
3	9	13	14

Grasp the Inverse Operation (p. 23)

11	8	2	5
13	4	15	1
12	9	7	10
3	14	6	16

Haul in Some Inverse Operations (p. 24)

7	12	2	9
3	1	6	8
13	4	5	16
11	14	15	10

Charge for the Quotient (p. 25)

7	1	5	15
2	10	13	8
12	3	16	11
4	14	9	6

A Quotient Sprint (p. 26)

4	13	8	12
10	1	14	6
16	7	2	9
11	3	15	5

Cart Off Some Quotients (p. 27)

6	16	13	1
8	11	9	10
2	15	3	14
12	4	7	5

Grapple for Some Quotients (p. 28)

5	12	9	16
10	3	1	7
15	8	14	2
13	4	11	6

Dive Into Challenging Division (p. 29)

2	11	15	12
6	4	8	9
3	13	16	5
7	14	10	1

Decimal Dash (p. 30)

8	9	5
4	11	6
7	1	3
12	14	13
15	2	10

Drag in Decimals on a Number Line (p. 31)

6	12	15
13	14	1
3	4	11
8	2	10
5	9	7

Nab a Product (p. 32)

6	1	8	7
3	15	4	16
10	12	11	9
5	14	2	13

Snare Decimal Multiples (p. 33)

1	7	2	11
15	8	6	12
14	3	16	4
9	10	13	5

Snap Up Change (p. 34)

6	12	4	10
15	1	16	8
7	14	2	11
3	9	13	5

Earn Some Decimals (p. 35)

16	4	15	8
12	7	2	13
1	6	9	10
3	11	14	5

Get Ready to Nab Decimals on a Number Line (p. 36)

14	7	3
15	1	13
9	11	5
2	8	10
6	12	4

Swoop Up Rounding Decimals (p. 37)

5	1	13
8	12	2
3	15	11
10	14	9
6	4	7

Reap Rounding Decimals to the Hundredths (p. 38)

2	13	7
14	1	15
8	12	10
4	11	3
6	9	5

Rack Up Rounding Decimals to the Thousandths (p. 39)

1	8	14
9	7	12
3	11	4
5	10	15
6	2	13

Sweep Up Decimals (p. 40)

9	1	6	3	7	11
10	4	12	8	2	5

Tag Some Ordered Decimals (p. 41)

5	12	10
14	8	4
1	15	7
11	3	13
6	9	2

Ambush Some Decimal Round-ups (p. 42)

14	1	15	9
7	11	3	16
2	8	13	5
6	12	4	10

Dive for Decimal Quotient Unknowns (p. 43)

11	3	12
6	13	5
9	7	4
2	15	10
14	8	1

Extract Some Decimal Division Estimations (p. 44)

11	1	4
2	13	10
14	3	8
5	7	15
9	12	6

Groove With Decimal Multiples (p. 45)

14	6	2
13	12	10
4	1	8
7	11	5
3	9	15

Factor Find (p. 46)

1	6	4	11
10	14	3	15
5	2	9	12
8	13	16	7

Grapple With Greatest Common Factors (GCF) (p. 47)

9	7	12	8
2	4	3	13
14	1	10	11
5	16	15	6

Clip Lowest Common Denominators (p. 48)

16	1	13	6
4	9	12	2
14	3	8	15
7	10	11	5

Conquest Over Common Denominators (p. 49)

3	9	2	4
12	1	16	6
11	7	8	14
5	10	13	15

Find an Improper Fraction (p. 50)

5	11	15	4
3	8	13	7
12	6	1	16
9	2	14	10

Hook Fractions as Part of a Collection (p. 51)

4	8	5	9
14	13	6	16
1	2	7	3
15	12	11	10

Lasso Fractions in a Collection (p. 52)

2	1	8	3
10	4	5	13
12	7	6	9
14	15	11	16

Reduce Those Fractions (p. 53)

11	16
4	8
14	1
9	6
3	15
5	13
7	12
2	10

Snatch the Least Common Multiple (p. 54)

2	5	14
15	3	13
7	11	1
8	4	10
12	6	9

Secure Some Fractions (p. 55)

7	13	1	10
9	2	12	5
3	15	6	14
16	11	4	8

Grasp a Fractional Location (p. 56)

5	11	12	4
15	3	8	9
13	7	2	16
1	10	14	6

Stamp Out Common Denominators (p. 57)

8	12	6
2	7	14
4	1	10
13	5	15
3	11	9

Triumph Over Adding Fractions (p. 58)

6	16	10	2
3	1	11	15
5	7	4	8
14	12	13	9

Bring in a Flood of Quotients (p. 59)

4	11	12	3
13	16	8	7
15	2	6	14
1	9	10	5

Win a Product (p. 60)

8	15	2
14	6	13
11	1	7
12	5	10
4	9	3

Conquer Multiplying Mixed Numbers (p. 61)

9	10	4	5
3	15	2	13
6	1	16	8
11	14	7	12

Finding Fractional Parts of Whole Numbers (p. 62)

10	7	16	11
3	1	12	5
4	15	2	9
13	8	14	6

Button Down Fractions and Decimals (p. 63)

11	7	9
4	8	2
5	1	12
15	10	6
13	3	14

Strike Out Some Mixed Numbers (p. 64)

8	10	23	4	13
24	1	17	9	20
5	18	2	21	14
12	19	3	16	7
25	6	22	11	15

Finding Fraction-Decimal Equivalents (p. 65)

4	9	12
6	11	2
3	7	14
13	1	15
8	5	10

Grab on to Fraction-Decimal-Percent Equivalents (p. 66)

10	8	5	3
4	11	13	1
12	14	6	15
2	9	16	7

Collar Some Multiples (p. 67)

13	6	16	4
5	3	11	9
8	12	10	14
1	15	2	7

Salvage Lots of Percent Equivalents (p. 68)

9	6	13	11
7	16	3	2
12	1	15	8
4	10	5	14

Pounce on a Percent (p. 69)

7	12	11	4
2	16	1	14
9	3	15	8
10	6	13	5

Round Up Percents (p. 70)

9	1	10
5	14	4
12	3	8
13	15	11
2	6	7

Snare Sale Prices (p. 71)

6	3	14	9
11	8	16	5
4	13	2	12
1	10	15	7

Tag the Percent One Number Is of Another Number (p. 72)

9	6	11	16
8	2	13	5
3	14	1	10
15	4	7	12

Wrap Up a Raise (p. 73)

13	10
6	16
4	15
3	14
8	1
7	11
9	2
5	12

Draw in Ratios (p. 74)

10	8	6
9	1	14
13	3	2
4	11	5
15	7	12

Rack Up Ratios (p. 75)

13	9	5
11	14	8
7	2	12
3	10	4
15	1	6

Conquer Positive and Negative Numbers (p. 76)

14	10	1
2	11	7
9	6	12
5	8	3
13	4	15

Mark Some Positive and Negative Numbers (p. 77)

8	13	3
10	11	5
2	1	14
6	9	7
4	15	12

Pocket Positive and Negative Solutions (p. 78)

5	9	7	3
4	11	16	13
8	6	14	2
1	12	15	10

Hook Some Patterns (p. 79)

7	13	15	3
6	2	12	16
1	8	10	11
5	9	4	14

Pick Up a Numerical Pattern (p. 80)

12	10	14	5
2	15	13	11
4	9	1	7
6	8	16	3

Nab an Expression (p. 81)

3	15	10	6
4	2	8	12
11	1	13	9
5	7	16	14

Dance Away With Algebraic Expressions (p. 82)

6	15	9
11	1	13
4	12	3
2	10	7
8	5	14

Peg Some Algebraic Equations (p. 83)

1	12	6	14
2	8	3	15
5	10	4	13
11	9	16	7

Glide Through Algebraic Equations (p. 84)

14	4	15	3
10	11	16	2
8	7	12	9
1	13	6	5

Hook Algebraic Unknowns (p. 85)

16	1	15	12
6	14	2	8
7	3	9	11
5	13	4	10

Zip Away With Algebraic Expressions (p. 86)

9	1	16	11
6	12	13	5
14	2	8	10
4	7	15	3

Button Down the Cummutative Property (p. 87)

2	3	10
8	5	13
9	11	6
14	7	4
15	1	12

Draw in the Distributive Property (p. 88)

9	13	12
11	2	10
4	15	7
14	5	3
1	8	6

Douse the Density Property (p. 89)

14	15	6
1	10	13
7	2	4
12	11	9
5	8	3

Overcome Exponents (p. 90)

14	1	3	12
6	13	10	4
7	11	5	16
8	2	15	9

Latch on to Square Root Estimations (p. 91)

14	6	1
8	9	12
4	2	7
11	3	13
10	15	5

Search for a Square Root (p. 92)

15	9	14
12	4	1
10	2	5
11	7	8
6	3	13

Strike Out Square Roots (p. 93)

10	5	14
6	2	15
8	12	3
1	9	13
7	4	11

Pounce on Proportions (p. 94)

3	8	11
9	14	7
12	2	15
6	13	5
4	10	1

Crush Customary Units (p. 95)

12	3
16	9
7	14
10	1
8	2
15	5
4	13
6	11

Swap Customary Units (p. 96)

11	16
3	9
4	7
15	6
10	14
1	12
2	8
13	5

Tackle Metric Measurement (p. 97)

13	14
3	5
6	8
10	4
16	1
12	7
11	15
2	9

Munch Some Metrics (p. 98)

10	14
8	7
4	13
11	1
12	6
5	15
2	9
16	3

Lasso Lines and Points (p. 99)

8	13	15	3
9	1	11	2
5	6	12	16
7	4	14	10

Search for the Geometric Gold (p. 100)

9	15	3	16
11	1	7	13
5	10	6	2
8	14	4	12

Play With Perimeters (p. 101)

10	8	4
3	1	7
6	11	12
5	9	2

Buffalo Some Triangular Perimeters (p. 102)

3	10	1
14	5	6
13	9	11
7	4	2
15	12	8

Reach for Rectangular Areas (p. 103)

4	8	5
7	2	15
10	3	11
9	6	14
12	13	1

Latch on to Areas (p. 104)

8	6	11
2	4	9
10	7	1
12	5	3

Latch on to Two-Dimensional Areas (p. 105)

7	10	6	13
14	8	12	9
15	1	5	11
2	3	16	4

Crunch the Area of Triangles (p. 106)

4	16	6	11
8	1	15	2
13	12	3	10
9	5	14	7

Dive Into Triangular Areas (p. 107)

6	12	7
15	1	14
11	13	10
4	3	2
8	9	5

Conquer Geometric Shapes (p. 108)

3	13	12
5	4	9
14	7	2
6	11	10
1	8	15

Stamp Out Surface Areas (p. 109)

8	11	3
6	1	14
2	15	12
4	13	7
10	5	9

Wangle Surface Areas (p. 110)

10	5	11
13	7	2
3	9	6
14	15	12
4	8	1

Volley for Volume (p. 111)

3	6	15
7	8	13
4	11	10
1	12	9
2	14	5

Snatch Geometric Patterns (p. 112)

12	2
14	16
4	1
15	10
6	7
3	11
8	5
9	13

Grapple Geometric Patterns (p. 113)

8	7
1	4
5	3
2	15
6	11
13	16
10	12
14	9

Master Coordinates (p. 114)

5	13	15	11	19
4	6	14	1	16
2	17	3	8	7
20	10	9	12	18

Grab a Coordinate (p. 115)

12	19	3	14	16	2
22	6	7	18	11	1
17	13	20	15	4	24
10	23	21	9	5	8

Grip Some Graphing (p. 116)

6	11	4
5	14	10
13	1	7
8	9	12
3	15	2

Lap Up Laps (p. 117)

10	3	12	4	8
1	2	13	5	15
6	9	7	14	11